How the OCEANS work

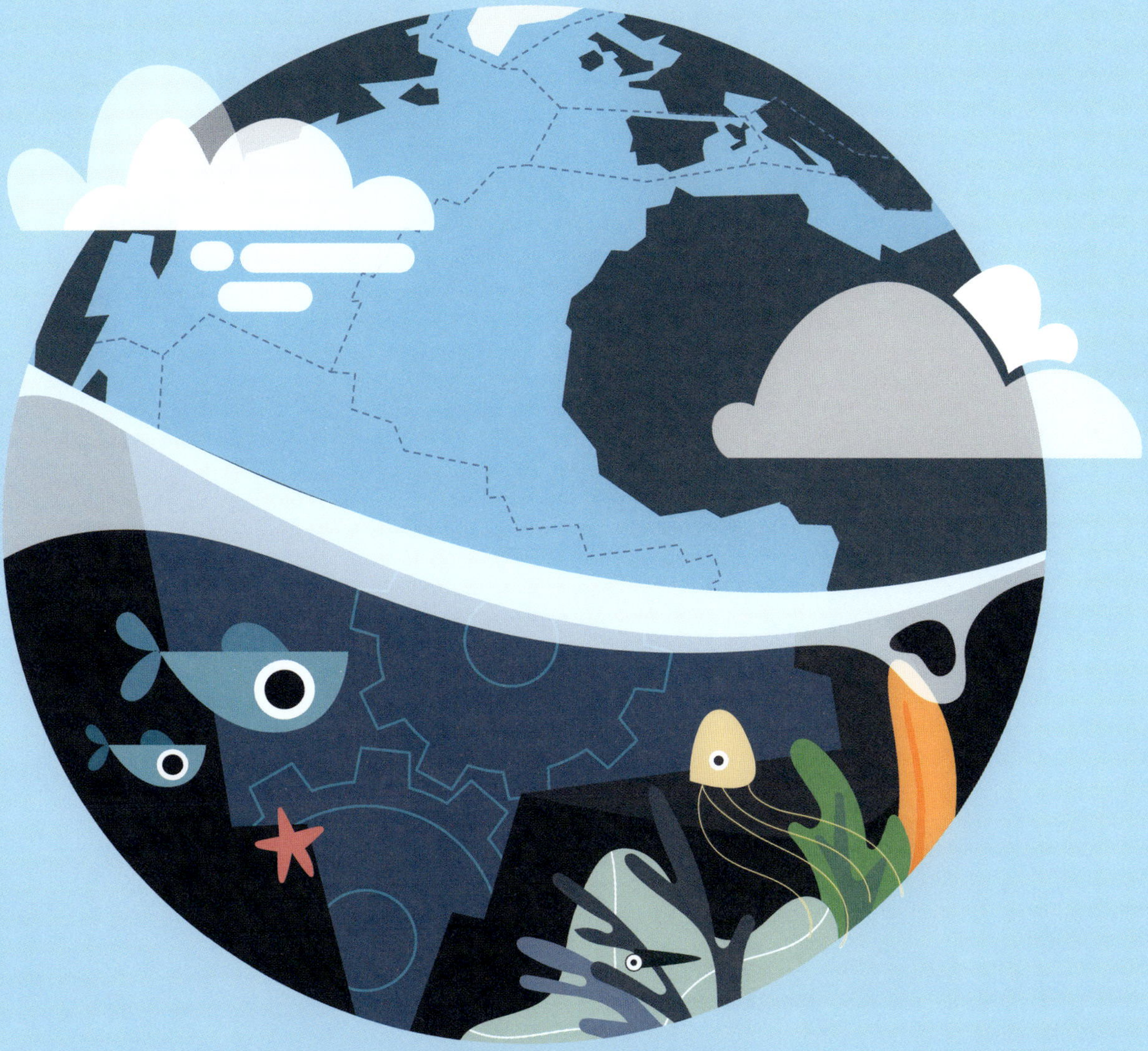

Dr Lucía Pérez Díaz

HOLA!

My name is Lucía, and I'm an Earth scientist. I study our planet the way a detective studies a mystery: by searching for clues left behind over billions of years. Just as people keep memories in photos, letters, or old objects, Earth keeps its own memories in rocks and landscapes. You just have to learn how to read them.

The oceans are Earth's greatest archive of information. Beneath the waves, the ocean floor is like a time machine, allowing scientists to travel back and explore in order to uncover how our planet once looked, how its surface shifted, and how the world we know today came to be. From the moment the first oceans formed, they have shaped Earth's climate, its landscapes, and the possibility of life itself. However, every answer scientists uncover leads to new questions.

This book invites you to explore what we know, and to imagine what we have yet to discover. That is the best part of being a scientist—knowing that there are always new mysteries waiting, and new stories Earth has been holding on to, just for someone curious enough to find them.

Are you ready to dive in?

Lucía

CONTENTS

BEFORE WE START

Water is everywhere on Earth, and it is always moving. Its journey is called the water cycle and it is one of Earth's most essential processes. It moves water across the planet, making it available to every living thing and helps shape the planet's climate.

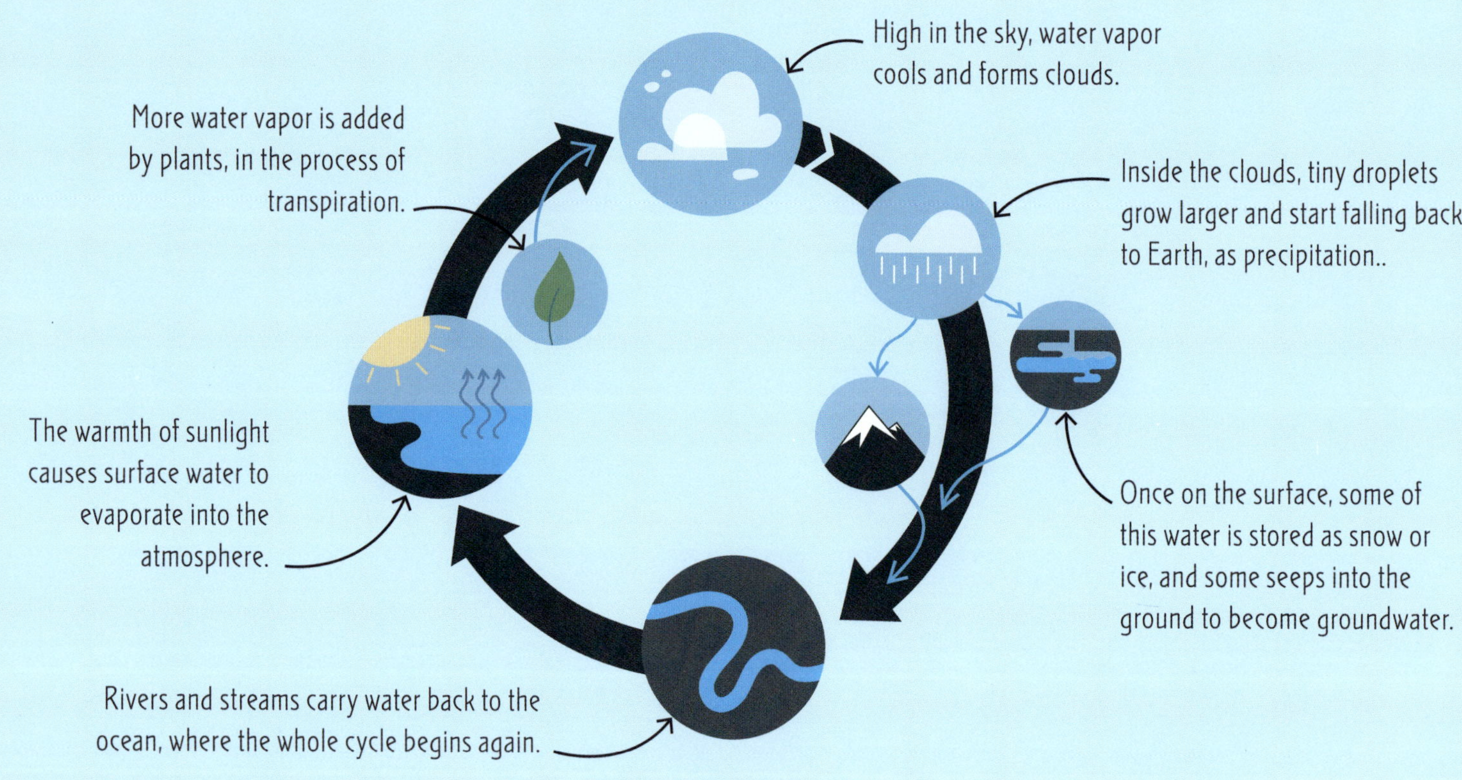

This cycle has been running for billions of years, almost as long as Earth has existed. The first liquid water appeared around 4.4 billion years ago and ever since, the same water has been endlessly recycling—shaping landscapes, sustaining life, and connecting every part of the planet.

Water stored
in the atmosphere
Precipitation
Water stored as
snow and ice
Transpiration
Evaporation
Water stored as
groundwater

A BLUE PLANET

Earth is often called the "blue planet," and if you look at it from space you can see why. Roughly 71 percent of our planet's surface is covered by water, about 97 percent of which is ocean. This makes our planet look like a shiny, blue marble, shimmering under the sun.

That's a lot of water on Earth—about 353 quintillion gallons (1,336 quintillion liters). To realize how big this number is, let's look at it like this: a thousand billions is a trillion; a thousand trillions is a quadrillion; a thousand quadrillions is a quintillion!

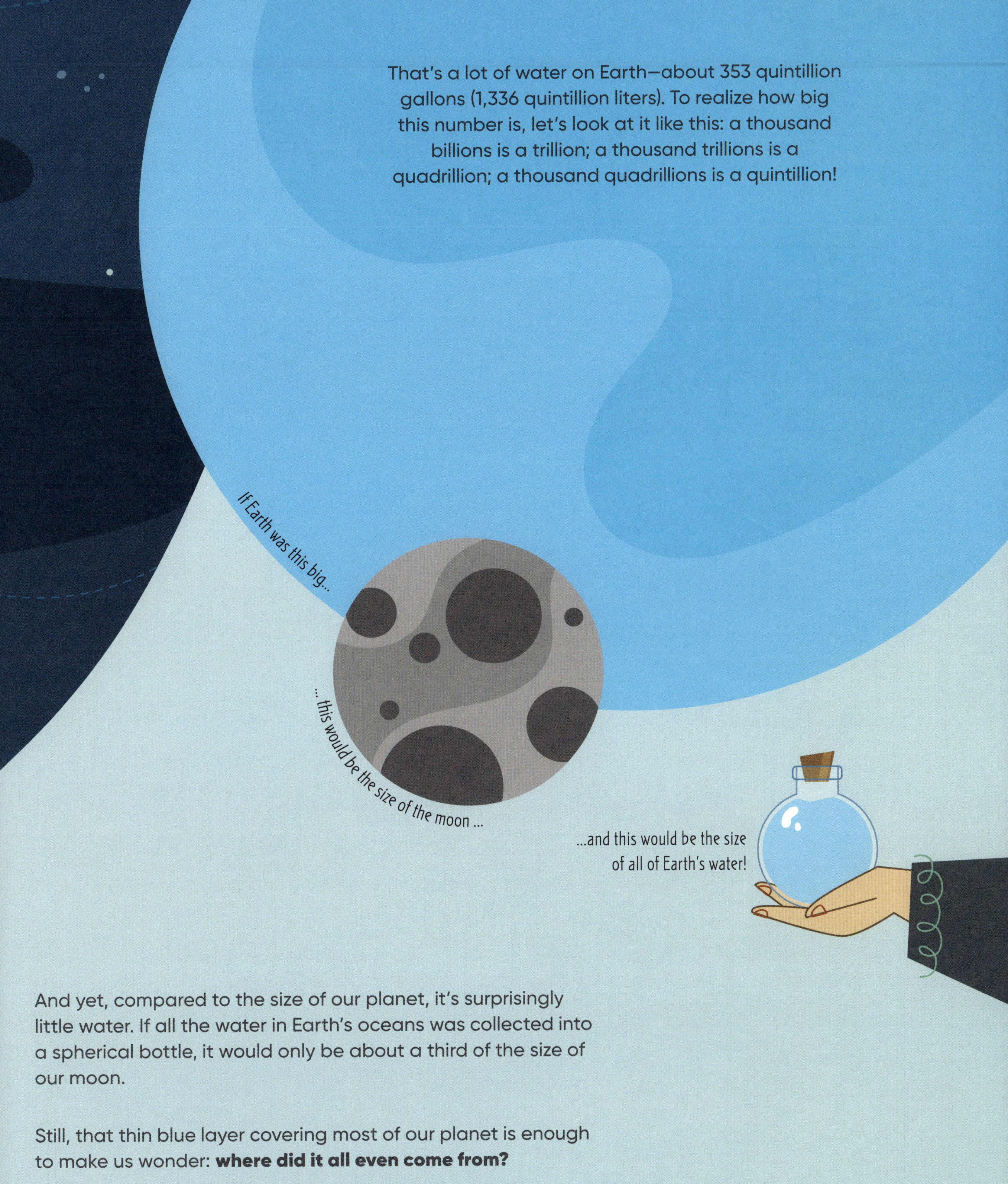

And yet, compared to the size of our planet, it's surprisingly little water. If all the water in Earth's oceans was collected into a spherical bottle, it would only be about a third of the size of our moon.

Still, that thin blue layer covering most of our planet is enough to make us wonder: **where did it all even come from?**

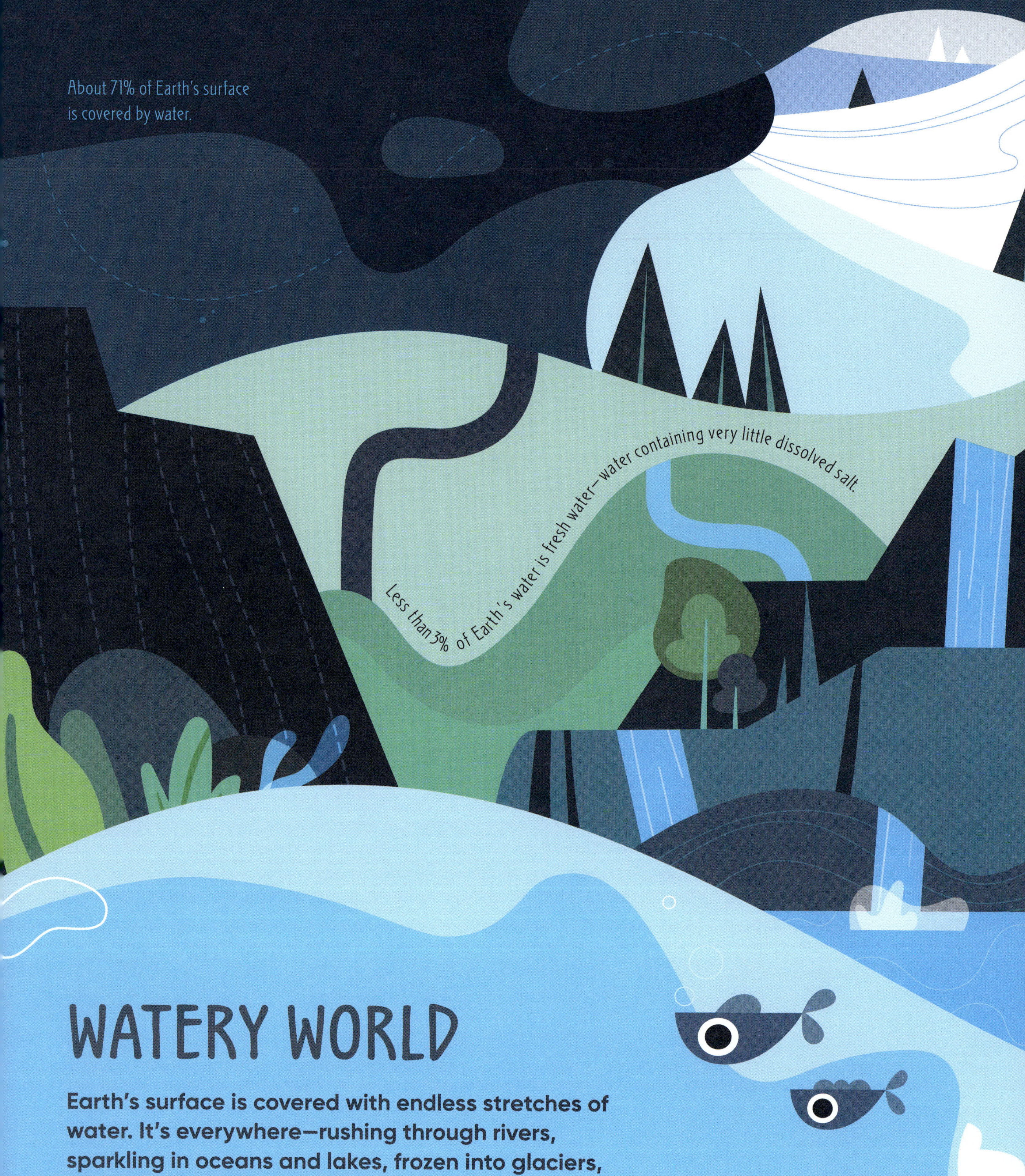

WATERY WORLD

Earth's surface is covered with endless stretches of water. It's everywhere—rushing through rivers, sparkling in oceans and lakes, frozen into glaciers, and drifting above us in clouds.

Mars, our dusty red neighbor, holds only frozen water locked in its poles. Elsewhere in our solar system, water is even harder to find. So how did all of our water get here? And how has Earth held onto it for billions of years, where other planets seem to have failed?

BACK TO THE BEGINNING

About 4.6 billion years ago, Earth had not formed yet, and just a cloud of gas and dust was orbiting around the newly formed sun. Particles of different sizes orbited the sun at slightly different speeds, allowing them to bump into each other and stick together. They grew bit by bit, from grains to pebbles to boulders, and eventually formed each of the four rocky planets.

At 4.6 billion years old, Earth might seem quite old... but if you compare it to the age of the universe (13.8 billion years old) it turns out that our planet is still fairly young!

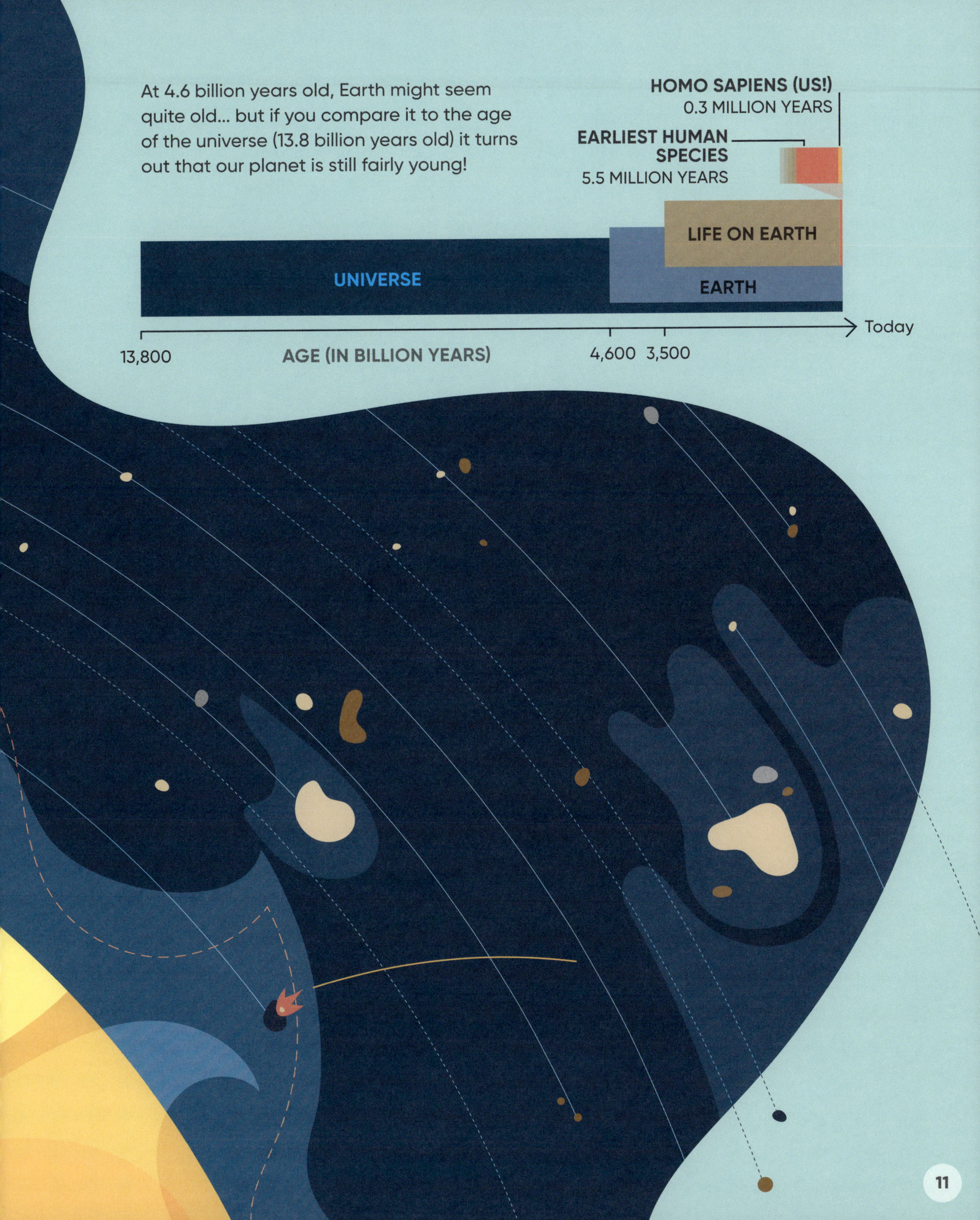

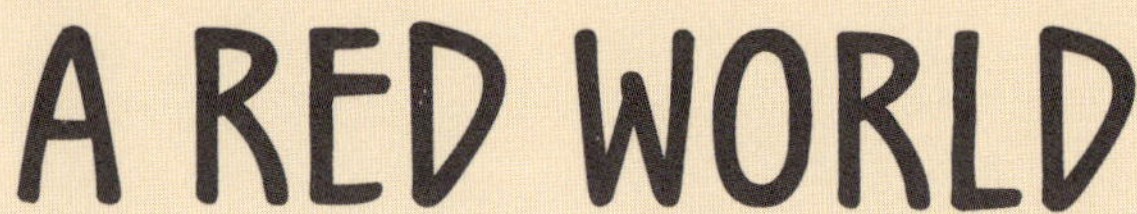

A RED WORLD

Baby Earth was not blue at all. It was red hot, glowing with heat from all of the impacts and collisions that resulted in its formation. The landscape was full of fiery volcanoes, erupting under a stormy and dark sky. Earth did have one ocean... or, rather, Earth was an ocean. An ocean made of magma—liquid rock.

Earth's early atmosphere had no oxygen, but lots of methane, ammonia, water vapor, carbon dioxide, and hydrogen.

WATER FROM FIRE?

Where exactly water came from, and when exactly our planet went from glowing red to shimmering blue, is not easy to know for sure. For a long time, Earth scientists thought that water may have come from space, carried by comets or asteroids that smashed into the young planet. But there is another idea: perhaps Earth made its own water from ingredients stored within the planet itself.

Earth's early surface was covered in bubbling magma, and its atmosphere had a lot of a gas called hydrogen. It is possible that the conditions were just right for a chemical reaction to occur, one that produces water.

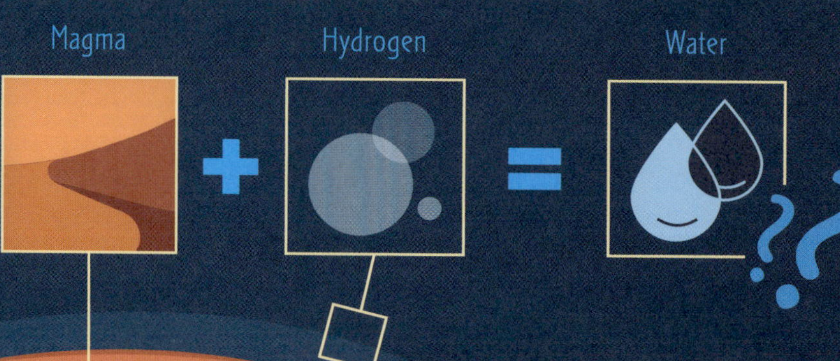

There's one thing we know for sure—there has been liquid water on Earth for at least 3.8 billion years. We know because of something called "pillow basalt," a type of rock that forms when lava erupts underwater. Of the millions of pillow basalts on the seafloor today, a small number have been found to be that old. Studies of some minerals called zircons suggest that water may have been around even earlier!

Pillow basalts

But here is a puzzle: if Earth's first oceans may have formed as far back as nearly four billion years ago, how is it possible that the oldest oceanic crust rocks we can find on Earth today are, at most, 250 million years old? To answer that question, you need to understand how oceans work.

A HOME FOR LIFE

If you are trying to build a planet that can support life, there is one thing you cannot do without: water.

That's because water is really good at taking part in all kinds of chemical reactions. All of the processes that sustain life rely on these chemical reactions, which means that all living things, no matter how big or small, need water in order to grow and survive.

If you are a rock floating in space, getting water is only the first step. Keeping it, and in liquid form, is the really tricky part.

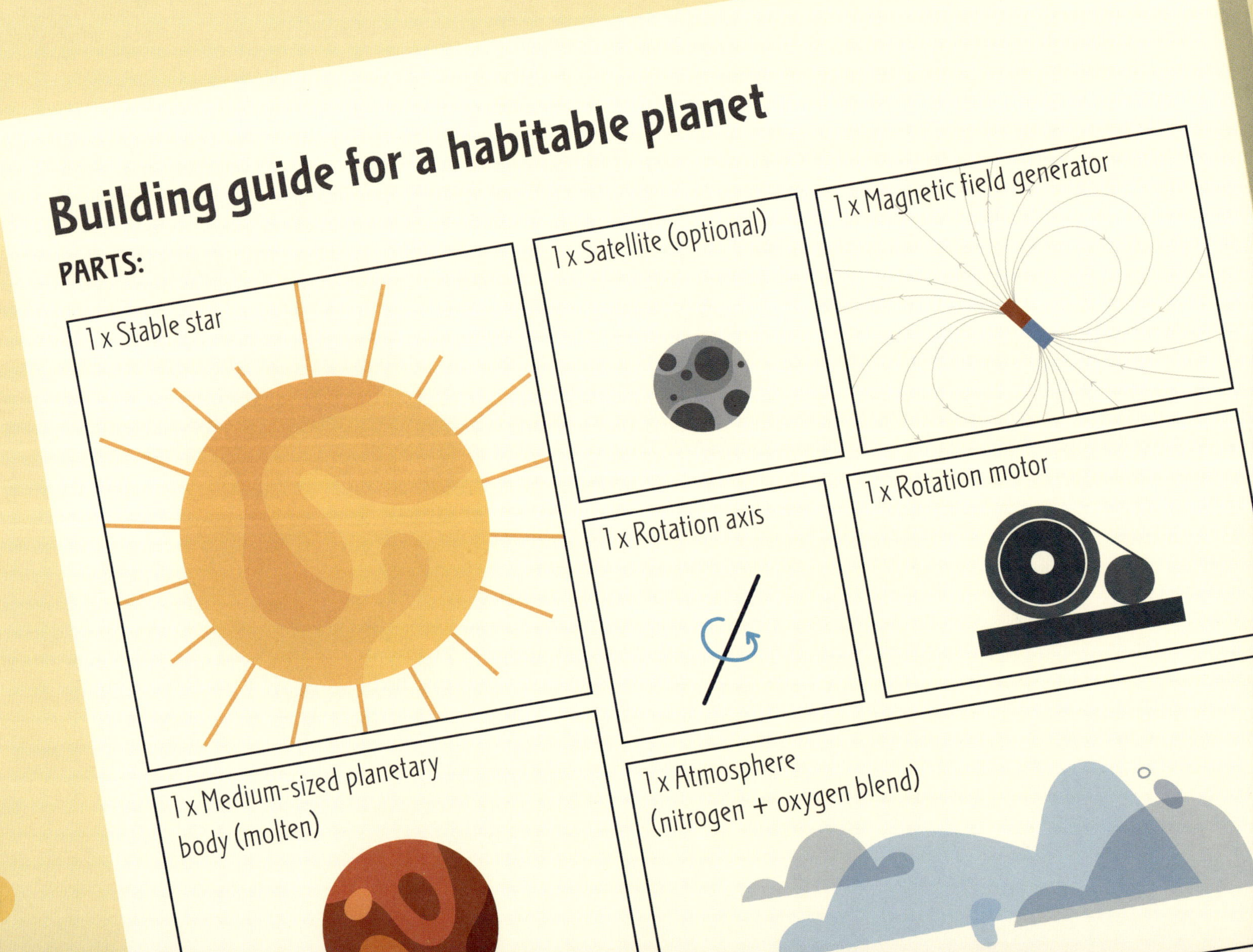

ASSEMBLY:

1 Place your planetary body near the star. Not too close, not too far.

Allow your planetary body to cool. It will become layered, with dense metals sinking into its center and forming a core.

2 Install the rotation axis and motor, for your planet to have days and seasons.

3 Install the magnetic field generator in your planet's newly formed core. It will protect your planet from harmful solar radiation.

4 Activate atmosphere for added protection—like a planetary blanket. At this stage, you can also add one (or more) satellites to orbit around your planet.

Add water... and wait for life!

NOTES:

1. If the planet is too close to its star, the magnetic field is too weak, or the atmosphere is overloaded with greenhouse gases, the surface may overheat and water will evaporate.

2. If the planet is too far from its star, or too small to hold onto a thick atmosphere, it may become too cold and the water will freeze.

Other rocky planets—like Mars—probably had water when they were young. But only Earth held onto liquid water for billions of years. That's partly thanks to its location: not too close to the sun, not too far. But it's also because Earth has two invisible shields: a magnetic field and a stable atmosphere, which help protect it from the sun's radiation and trap water near the surface.

ONE BIG OCEAN

Although Earth is split into five major oceans, you could technically say it has only one (really big) ocean, because they are all connected.

Each holds clues to Earth's past, but one in particular—the Atlantic Ocean—led scientists to one of the biggest breakthroughs in Earth science: the theory of plate tectonics.

ARCTIC OCEAN
PACIFIC OCEAN
INDIAN OCEAN

PUZZLE PLANET

The theory of plate tectonics tells us that the Earth's outer shell (the lithosphere, made of the crust and the very top of the mantle) is broken into giant pieces called tectonic plates. These plates are constantly moving, though slow enough that we cannot feel it—about as fast as your fingernails grow!

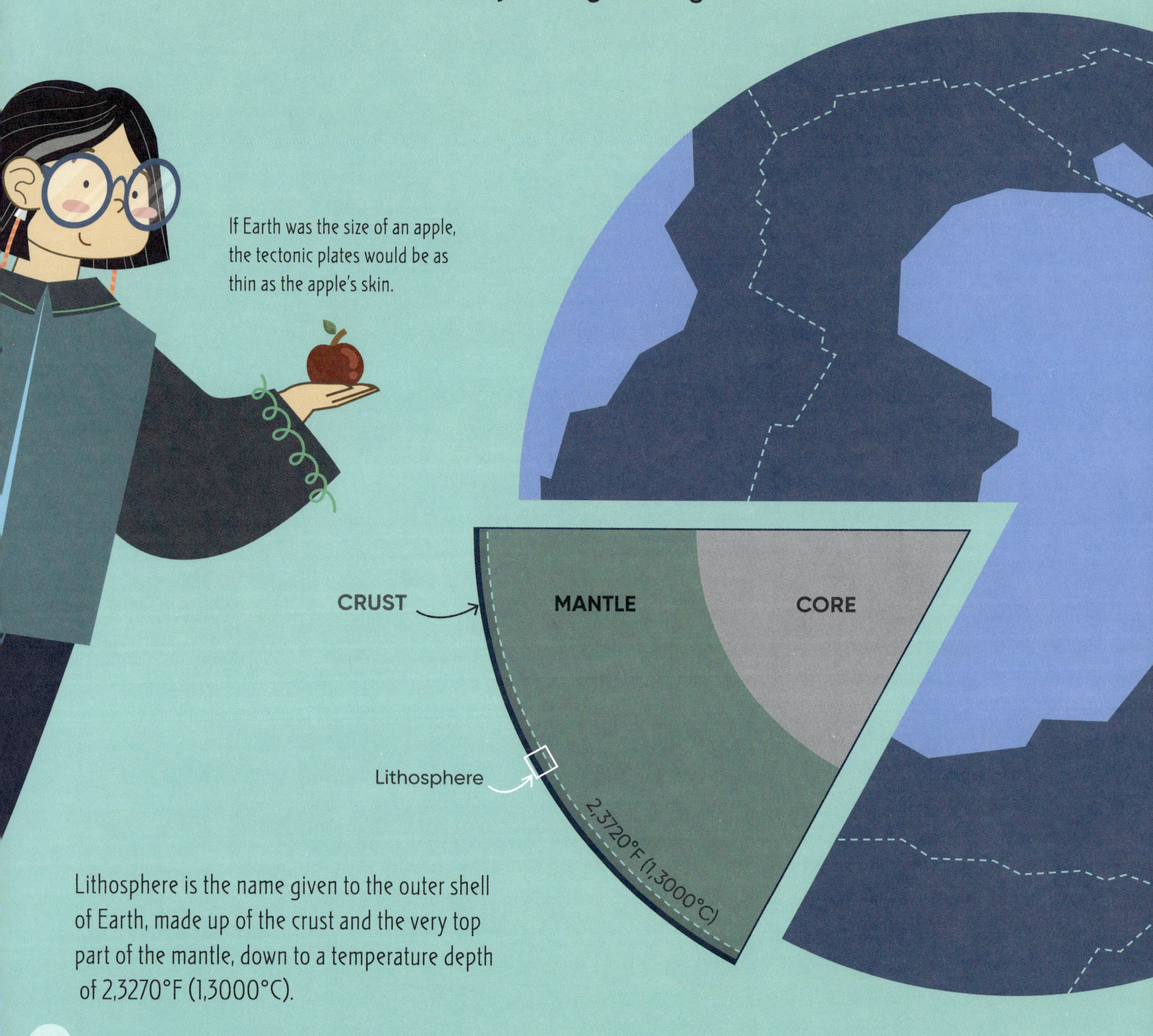

Lithosphere is the name given to the outer shell of Earth, made up of the crust and the very top part of the mantle, down to a temperature depth of 2,3270°F (1,3000°C).

The lithosphere is thinnest beneath the oceans, particularly near mid-ocean ridges. Along them, two tectonic plates are spreading apart, and oceanic lithosphere is only a few miles thick.

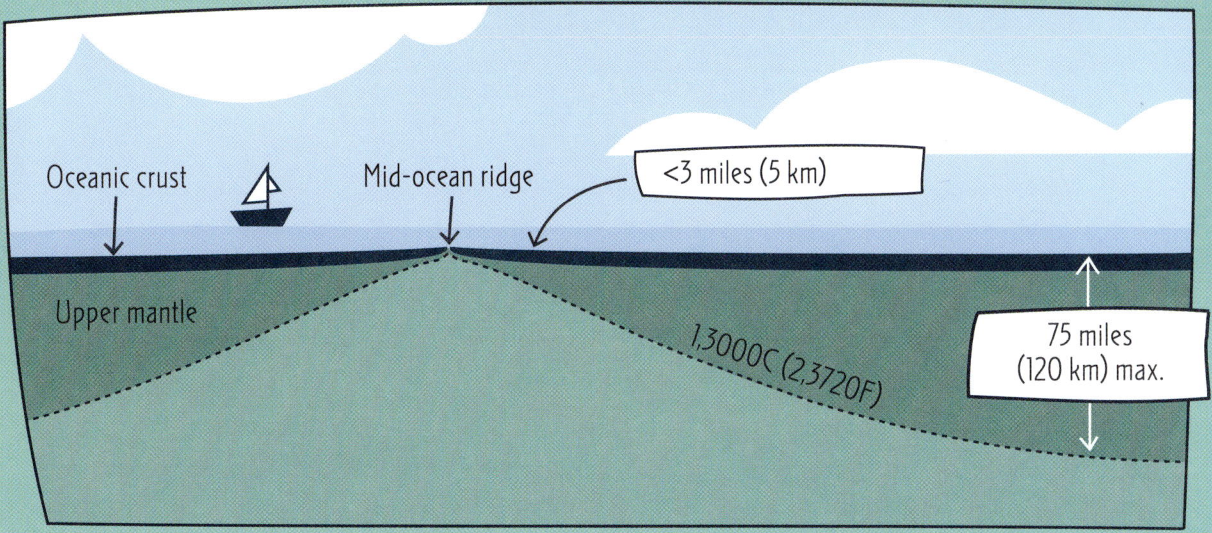

By contrast, it's thickest beneath continents. The base of continental lithosphere can be found hundreds of miles deep.

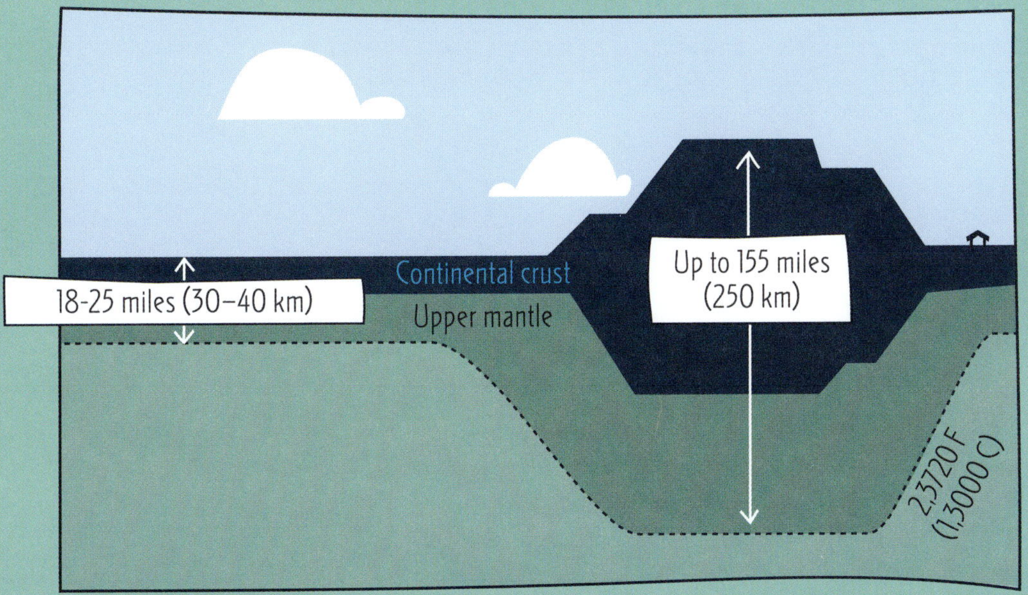

Some tectonic plates—like the African Plate—include both oceanic and continental regions, so even within a single plate, the lithosphere can vary greatly in thickness.

A CHANGING PLANET

Tectonic plates are always in motion, and have been for hundreds of millions of years. As they move, interesting things happen where the plates meet.

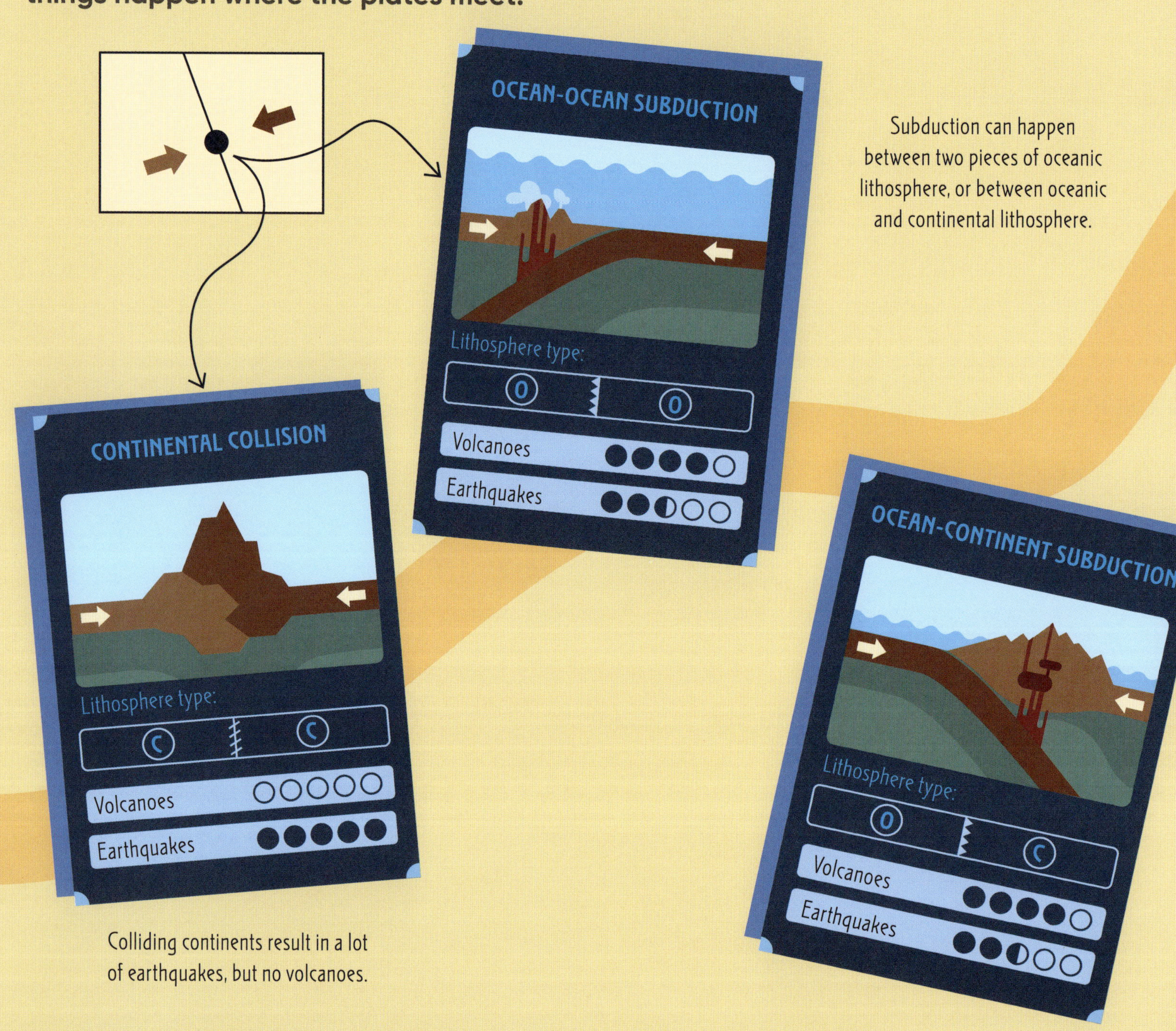

Subduction can happen between two pieces of oceanic lithosphere, or between oceanic and continental lithosphere.

Colliding continents result in a lot of earthquakes, but no volcanoes.

Boundaries between two plates that are moving toward each other are called "convergent" because two slabs of lithosphere are coming together. Colliding plates can crumple up into mountains, or plunge beneath one another in a process called "subduction," where lithosphere is recycled back into the Earth's mantle.

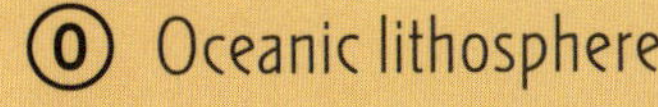

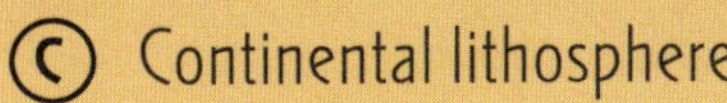

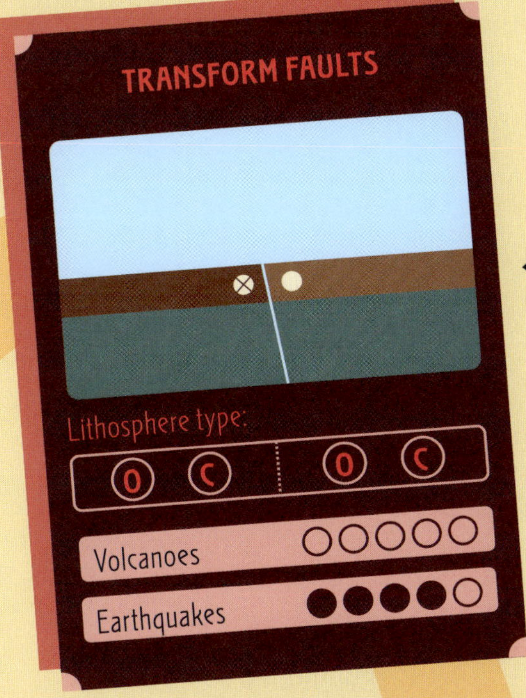

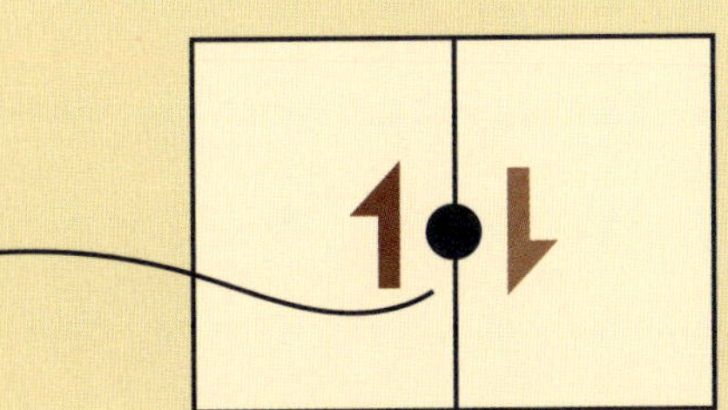

Other times, two tectonic plates may simply slide past each other. This is a "transform plate" boundary, where an area of lithosphere is neither created nor destroyed.

Divergent boundaries result in lots of volcanoes, but fewer earthquakes than along convergent boundaries.

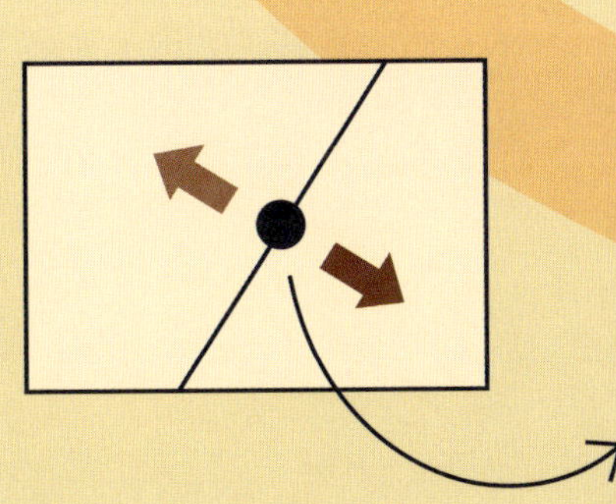

Lastly, plate boundaries can be "divergent," in places where two plates are pulling apart. Mantle rocks rise to fill in the space, and brand new lithosphere is created.

That is how new oceans form.

AN OCEAN FULL OF CLUES

The Atlantic Ocean was particularly helpful to scientists in figuring out the existence of plate tectonics, because some of the continents on either side of the ocean look like puzzle pieces that once fit together. First noticed by mapmakers many centuries ago, they initially thought it may just be a coincidence—how could something as massive as a continent break?

Then came Marie Tharp. In the 1950s, she used depth measurements collected by ocean research ships to draw maps of the Atlantic Ocean floor. She discovered a surprise: it wasn't flat.

Running down the middle of the Atlantic was a giant underwater volcano chain: the Mid-Atlantic Ridge. And a chain of volcanoes doesn't just exist in the Atlantic Ocean, but in every one of the world's oceans! These mid-ocean ridges mark places where tectonic plates are separating and mantle rocks are rising to fill the gaps, forming volcanoes as they do.

A CONTINENT BREAKS

Marie's discovery, combined with the similarities of continent coastlines, pointed strongly toward the possibility that Earth's outer layer must be broken into pieces that are constantly moving. It would still take some time for the theory of plate tectonics to be accepted, however, because nobody could quite explain how it's possible for something as huge as a continent to break.

Luckily, today we can actually see it happening.

SOUTH AMERICAN PLATE

The South Atlantic Ocean started just like East Africa today—with a single supercontinent, formed by South America and Africa, splitting into two.

In East Africa, the ground is cracking open. Volcanoes are appearing. Valley floors are sinking. The African Plate is breaking into two.

This process is called rifting, and in East Africa it started around 25 million years ago. If it continues (Earth can sometimes change its mind!), in about 10 to 20 million years, Africa's eastern edge will be completely separated from the rest of the continent, and ocean water will fill the space in between.

THE EAST AFRICAN RIFT

Today, East Africa shows rifting in action. In the northeast, seafloor has begun forming, while in the southwest, the lithosphere is only just beginning to crack. Across thousands of miles, we can see each stage of the process by which a continent breaks apart. It's like watching a super slow-motion magic trick. The Earth is changing right beneath our feet. Where a continent once was, an ocean will grow.

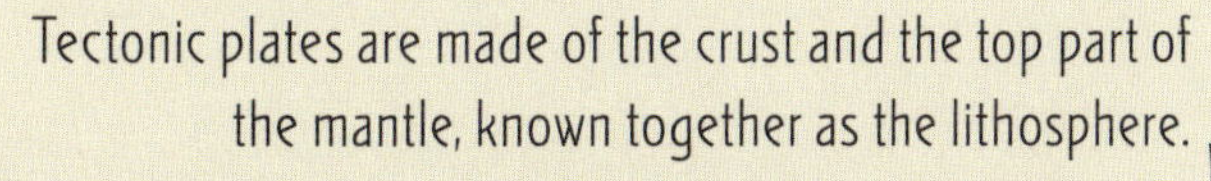

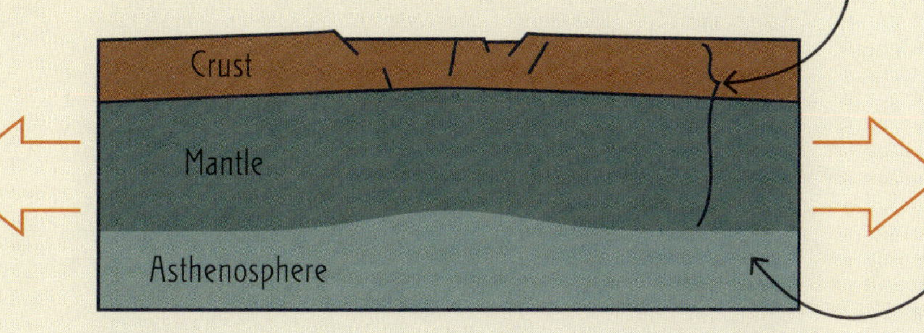

Tectonic plates move by gliding over the part of the mantle below the lithosphere: the asthenosphere.

Rifting doesn't happen all at once. It begins with small fractures in the crust—long, deep cracks where the land begins to sink.

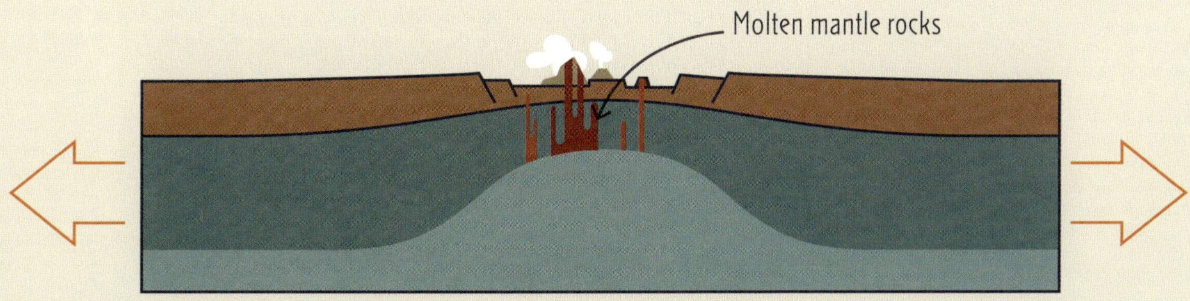

These grow into rift valleys, sometimes wide enough to see from space! As the lithosphere stretches thinner, the asthenosphere rises toward the surface, and something changes. When deep below, mantle rocks remain solid because they are under immense pressure, despite the high temperature. But, when mantle rocks are closer to the surface they are able to melt, rising to form volcanoes.

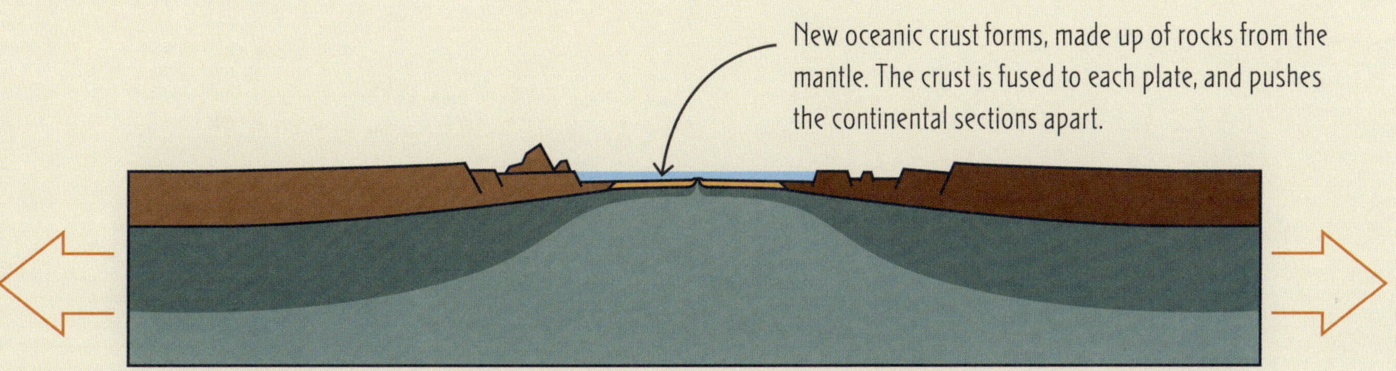

Eventually, if the rift keeps widening, the crust becomes so thin that it breaks completely. Molten mantle rocks erupt and become exposed at the surface, cooling and becoming solid. They aren't mantle rocks anymore, they now form brand-new oceanic lithosphere.

Or, in other words, **the very first seafloor of a new ocean is born.**

ROCKS THAT REMEMBER

Off the coast of East Africa, a new seafloor is only just beginning to form. But in other oceans, like the South Atlantic, the record stretches much further back.

At a mid-ocean ridge, where new crust is constantly forming, seafloor rocks are newborn, so zero million years old. To find older seafloor, you need to look closer to the continents. In the South Atlantic, they are around 140 million years old—that is how long ago seafloor between South America and Africa started to form.

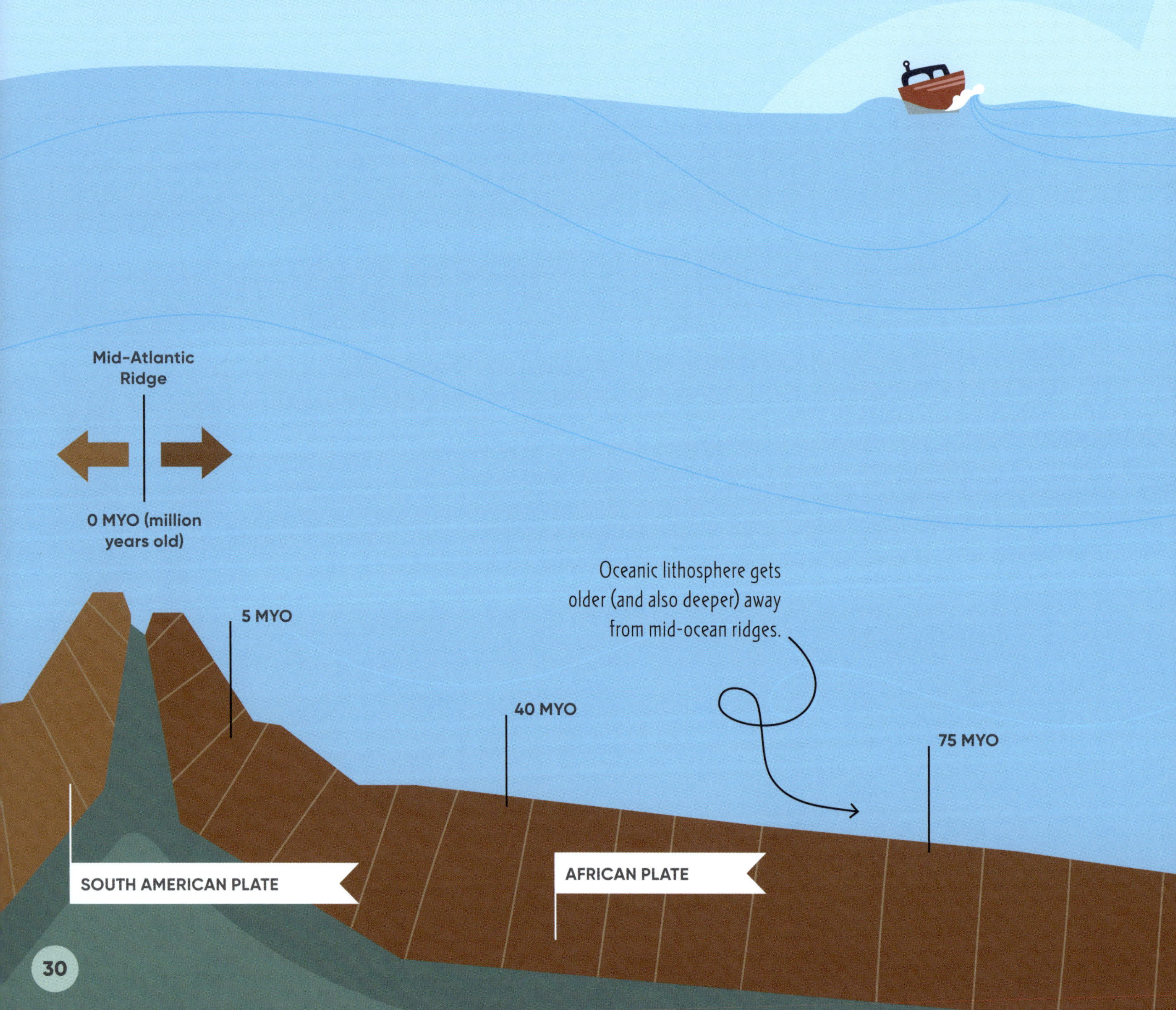

Normally, if you wanted to know how old a rock is, you would take a sample of it and study it in a lab. But, if that rock is under thousands of meters of water, even just collecting it would be quite a challenge. Luckily, the age of seafloor rocks can be read from afar, without ever even touching them.

This is possible because of **magnetism.**

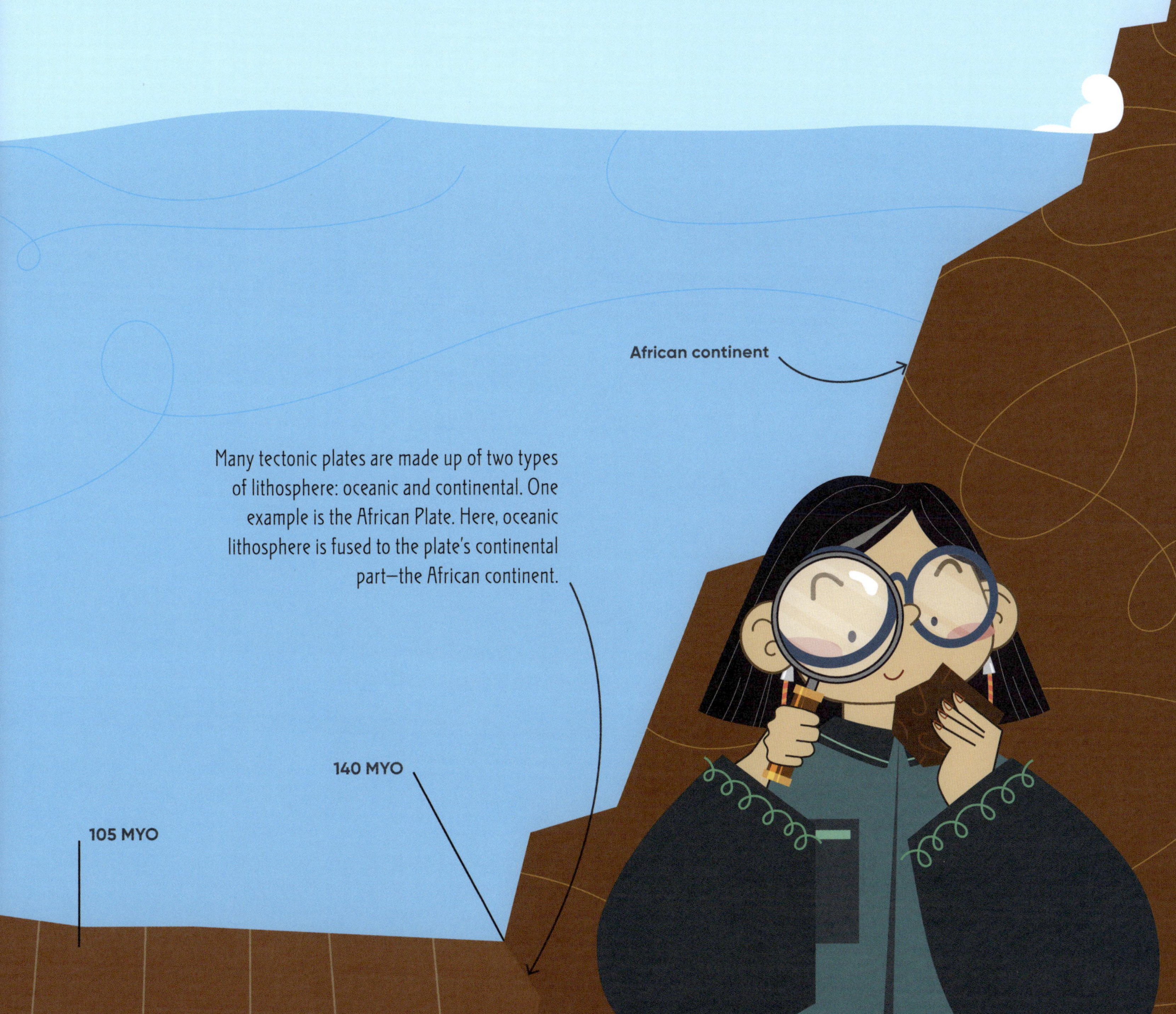

Many tectonic plates are made up of two types of lithosphere: oceanic and continental. One example is the African Plate. Here, oceanic lithosphere is fused to the plate's continental part—the African continent.

EARTH'S MAGNETIC FIELD

Earth has its own magnetic field that, today, enters the planet near the North Pole and outward again near the South Pole. This is called "normal" polarity.

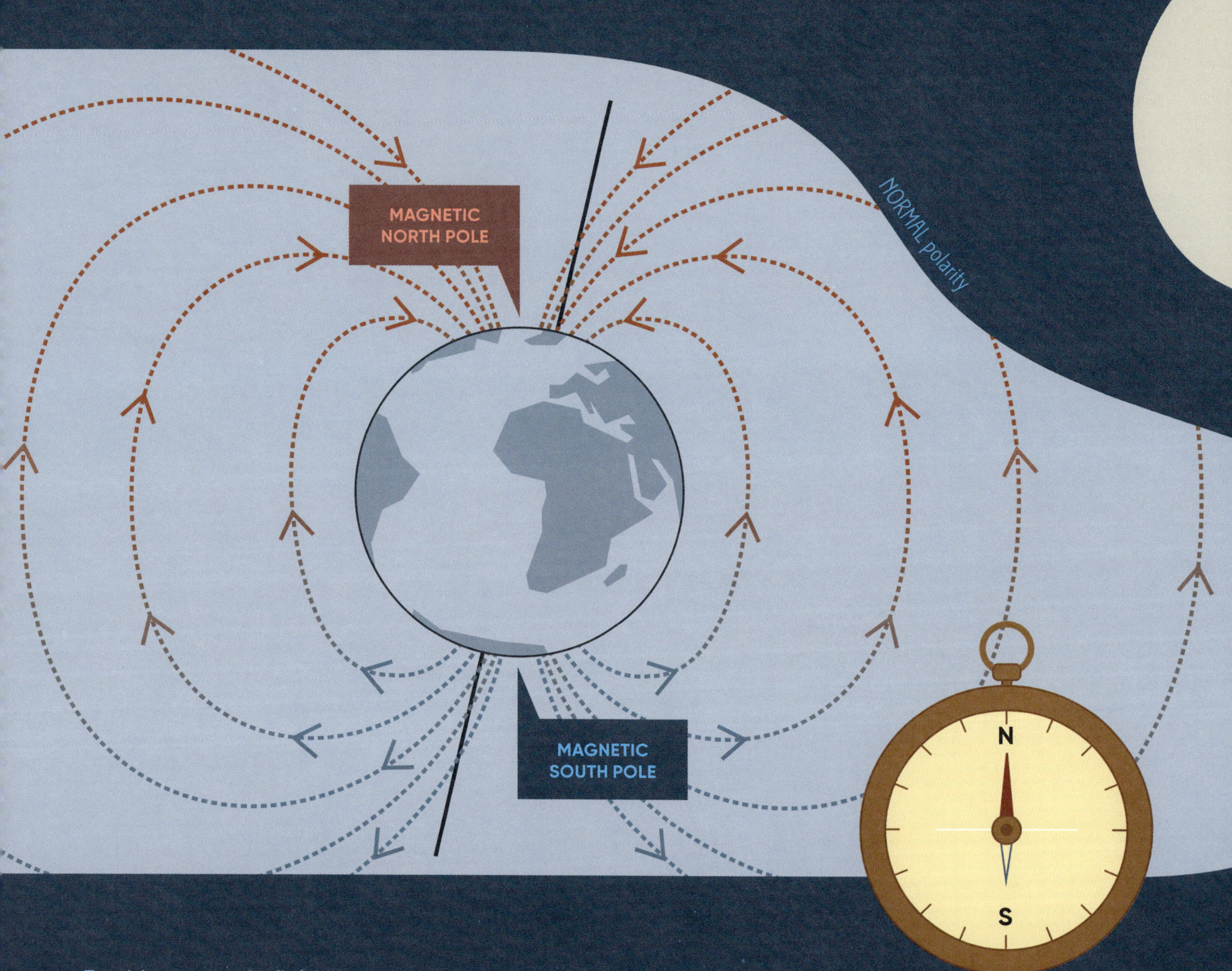

Earth's magnetic field is not, however, fixed. Many times in the past, **it has flipped.** Nobody knows why!

When it does, north becomes south, and south becomes north. This is known as "reverse" polarity. Sometimes these polarity reversals last only a short while. Other times, they last for millions or even tens of millions of years.

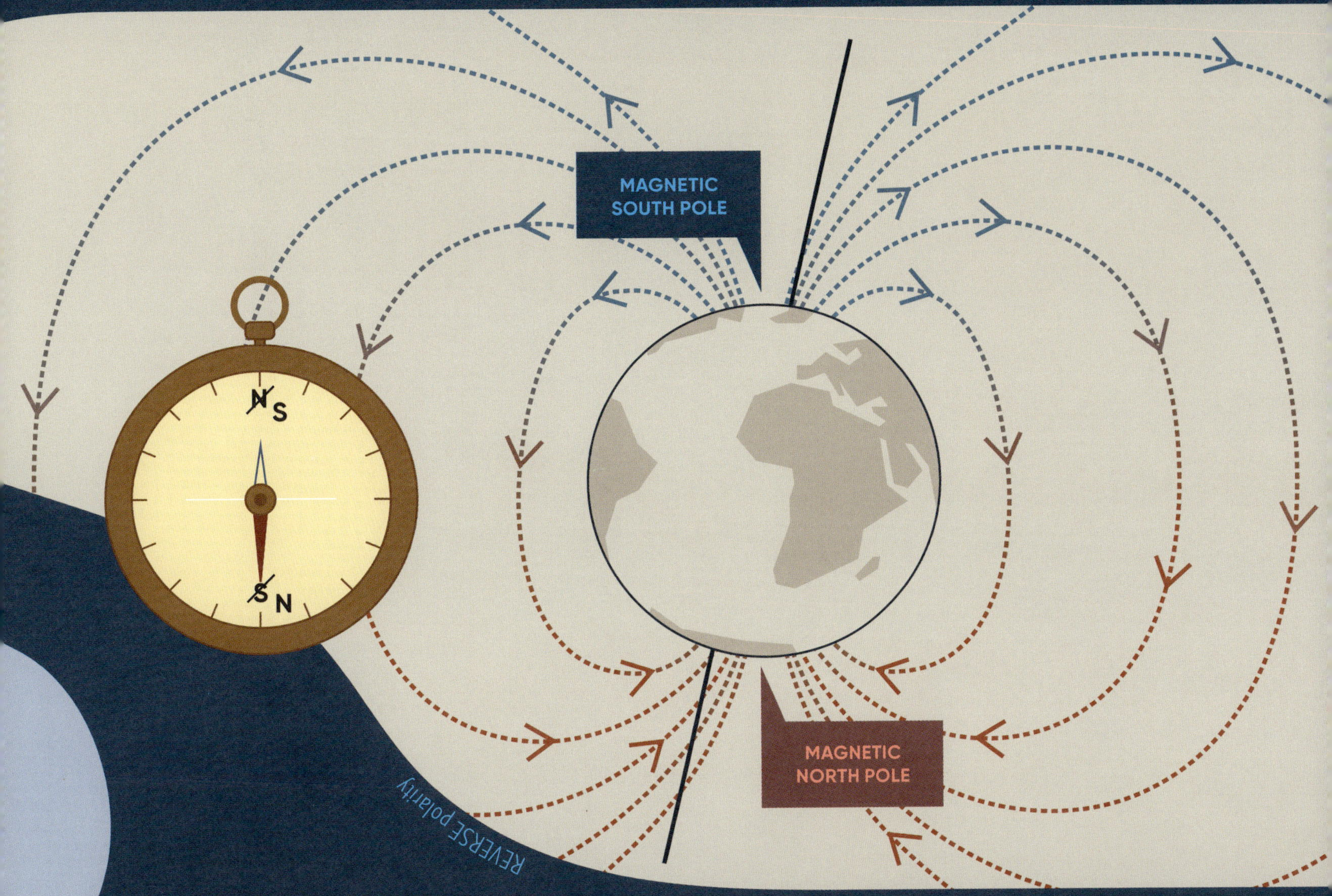

MAGNETIC SOUTH POLE

MAGNETIC NORTH POLE

REVERSE polarity

Any magnetic minerals inside rocks will always point to the magnetic North Pole. For example, when lava cools to form solid rock, the magnetic material inside that rock will point to whichever direction north is at the time.

The seafloor is made up of rocks with this **magnetic memory**. Some of their minerals point one way, and some point the other, depending on when the rock was formed.

The minerals in the rock cool down, to settle pointing north

AN INVISIBLE BARCODE

Over millions of years, new rocks form at mid-ocean ridges. They form in magnetic stripes which tell scientists the polarity of the Earth's magnetic field at that time—like a barcode of Earth's past! Because normal polarity is mapped in black and reverse polarity in white, they're sometimes called the "zebra stripes" of the seafloor.

The first ocean where zebra stripes were recorded was the East Pacific.

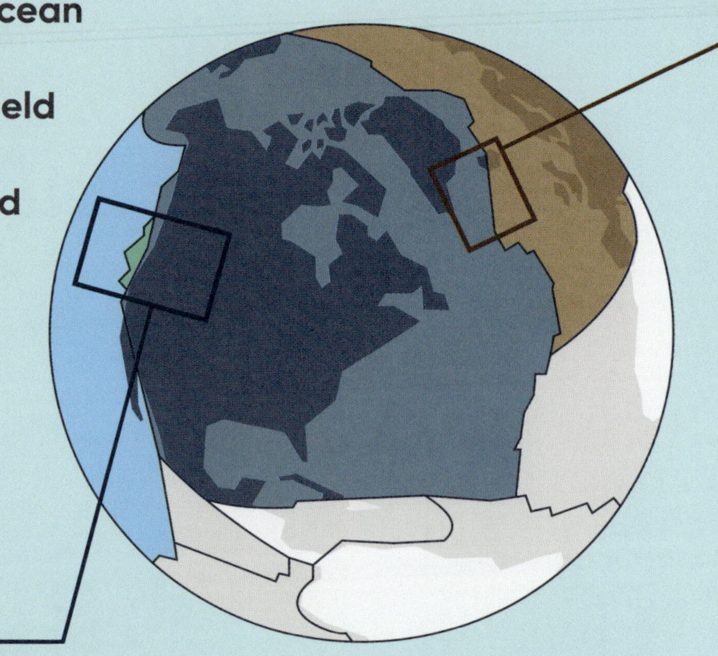

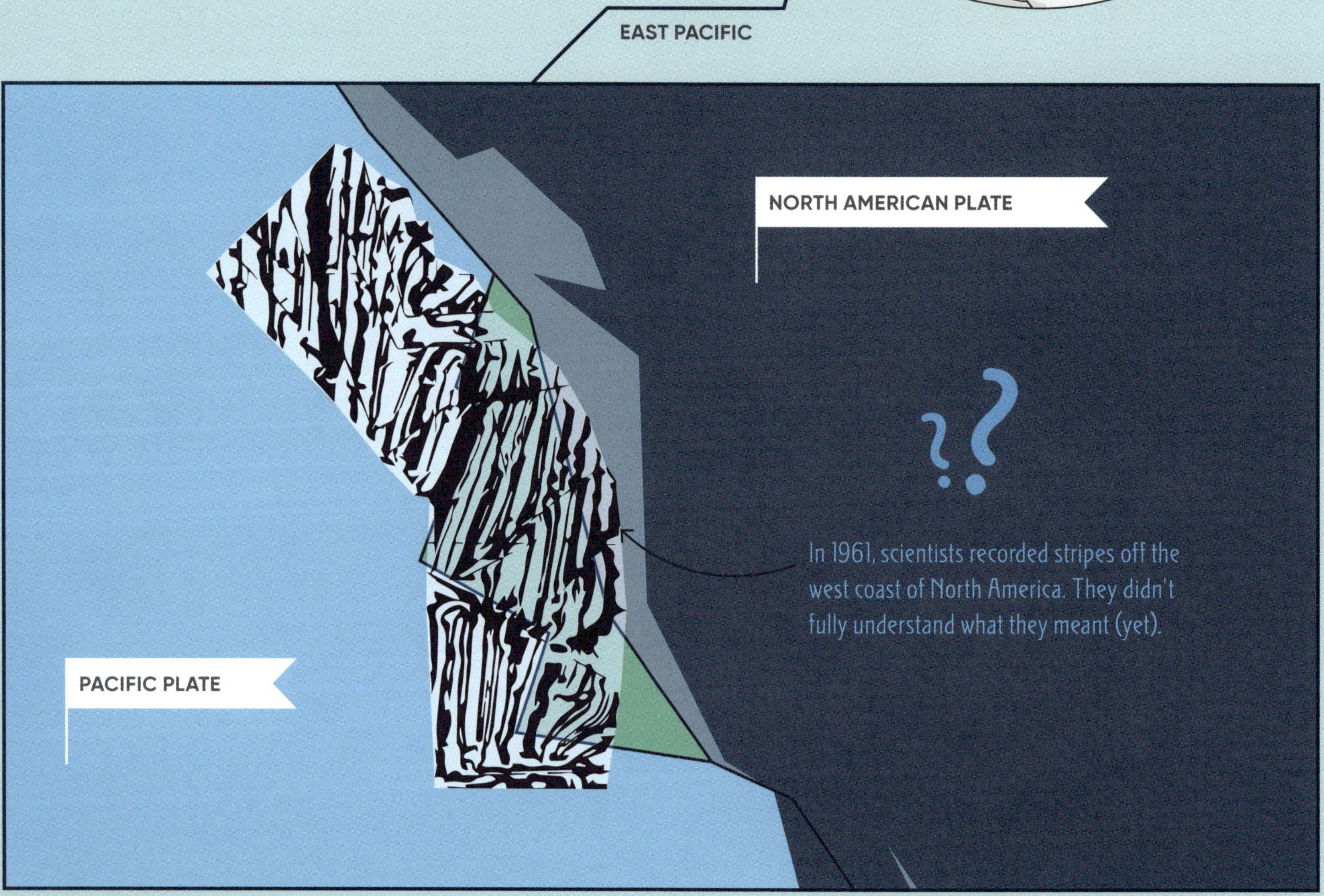

EAST PACIFIC

NORTH AMERICAN PLATE

PACIFIC PLATE

In 1961, scientists recorded stripes off the west coast of North America. They didn't fully understand what they meant (yet).

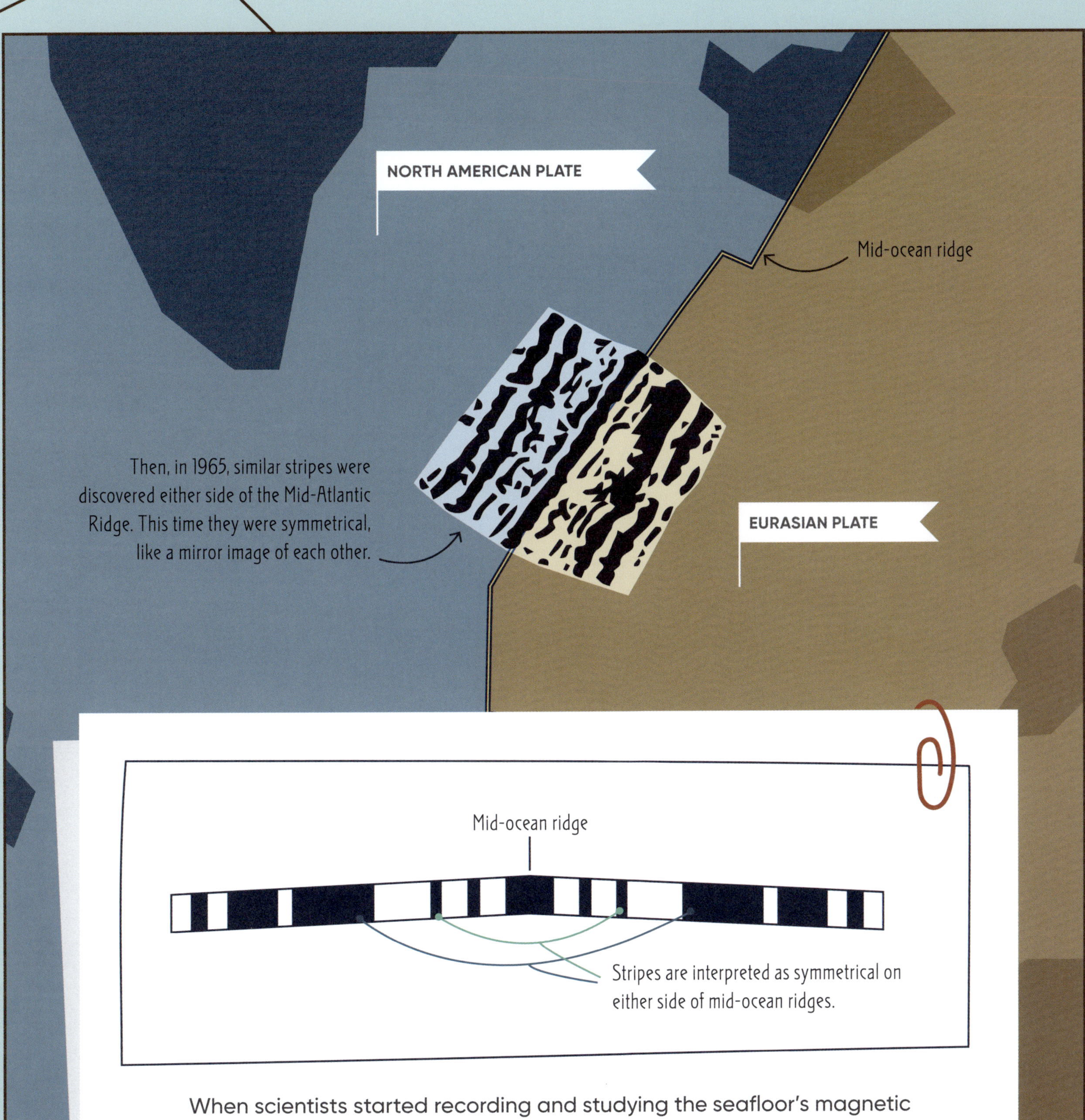

When scientists started recording and studying the seafloor's magnetic signals, they made two discoveries: they existed in every ocean, and they were mirror images on either side of mid-ocean ridges.

THE MAGNETIC CALENDAR

Volcanic lava, when it cools, captures and preserves the polarity of Earth's magnetic field. By dating thousands of lava flows and comparing which ones pointed north or south, scientists were able to build a timeline of polarity reversals throughout Earth's history.

When you have a lot of rock samples where you know both their age and polarity, you can build a timeline showing when magnetic flips have happened on Earth over the last several million years.

Each time the color changes is a moment when the magnetic field flipped:

This record is known as the geomagnetic timescale—a calendar of magnetic flips stretching back millions of years. Although a little odd looking, this special calendar would soon prove to be very useful for better understanding how oceans work.

SEAFLOOR SPREADING

By matching the seafloor stripes with the magnetic timeline from land, scientists could prove that new crust forms at mid-ocean ridges and is pushed outward in both directions, recording a mirrored magnetic barcode on either side.

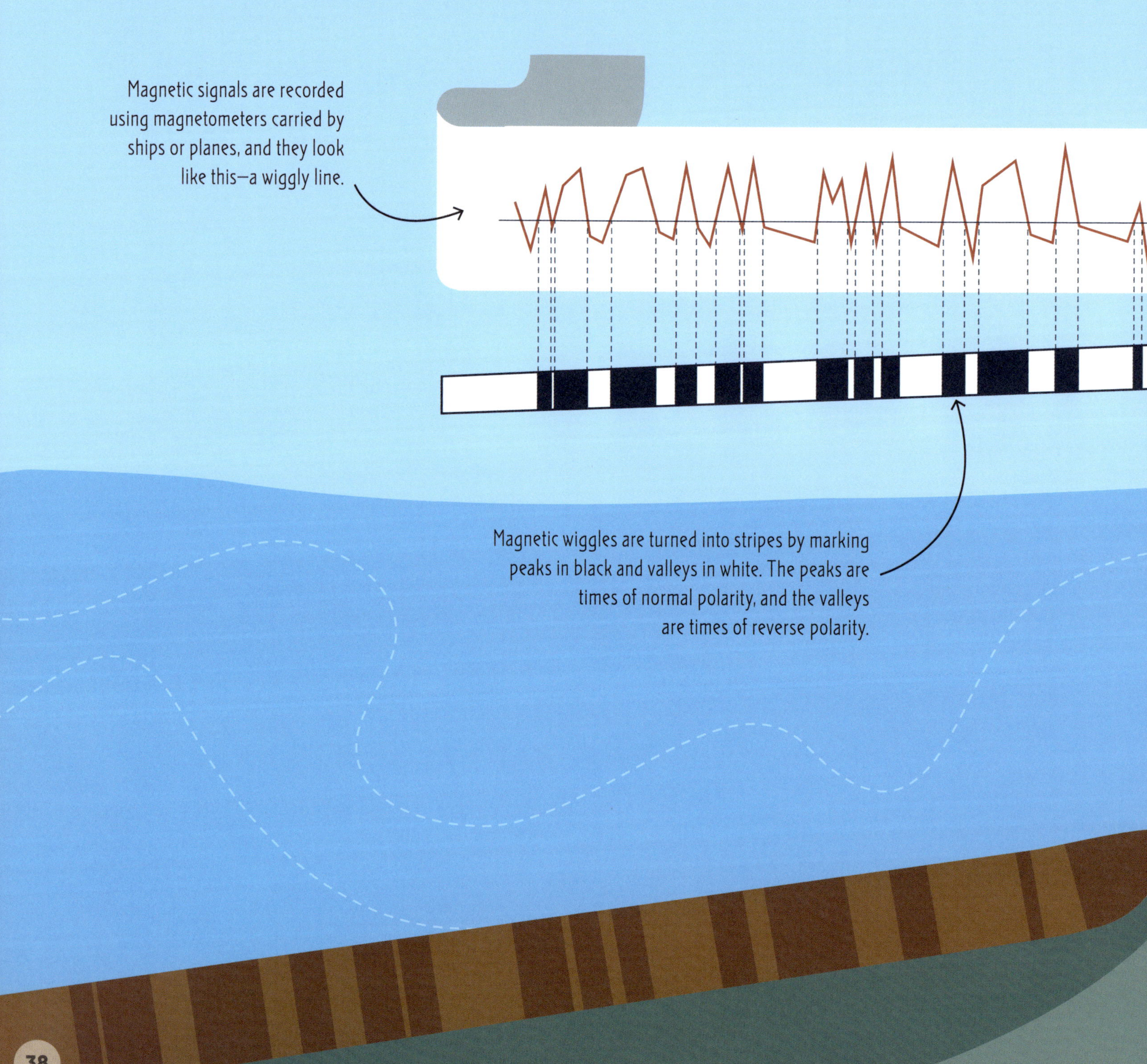

These magnetic patterns became a really important part of understanding plate tectonics, revealing that Earth's outer shell is in constant motion, and that the planet's past is written in the oceans themselves.

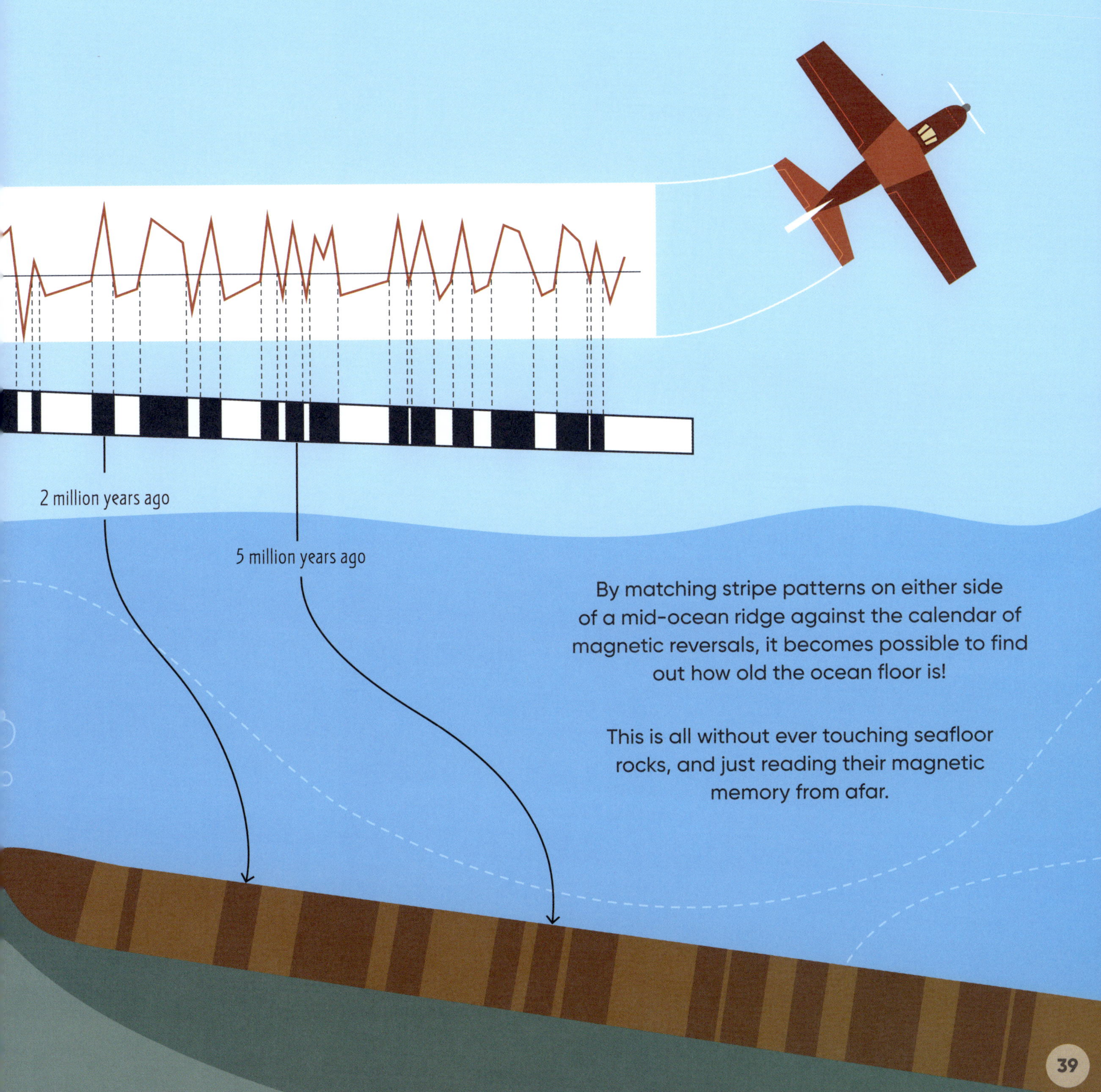

By matching stripe patterns on either side of a mid-ocean ridge against the calendar of magnetic reversals, it becomes possible to find out how old the ocean floor is!

This is all without ever touching seafloor rocks, and just reading their magnetic memory from afar.

SCARS OF TIMES GONE BY

Another clue about past plate movements comes from the "scars" that cross the ocean floor at sharp breaks across mid-ocean ridges.

Mid-ocean ridges aren't smooth lines. Instead, they are broken into segments with a steplike pattern. The breaks between the steps are called transform faults, and along them is where tectonic plates slide past each other. Over time, these movements leave long scars on the seafloor, called fracture zones. This record makes it possible to tell which direction the plates long ago moved in.

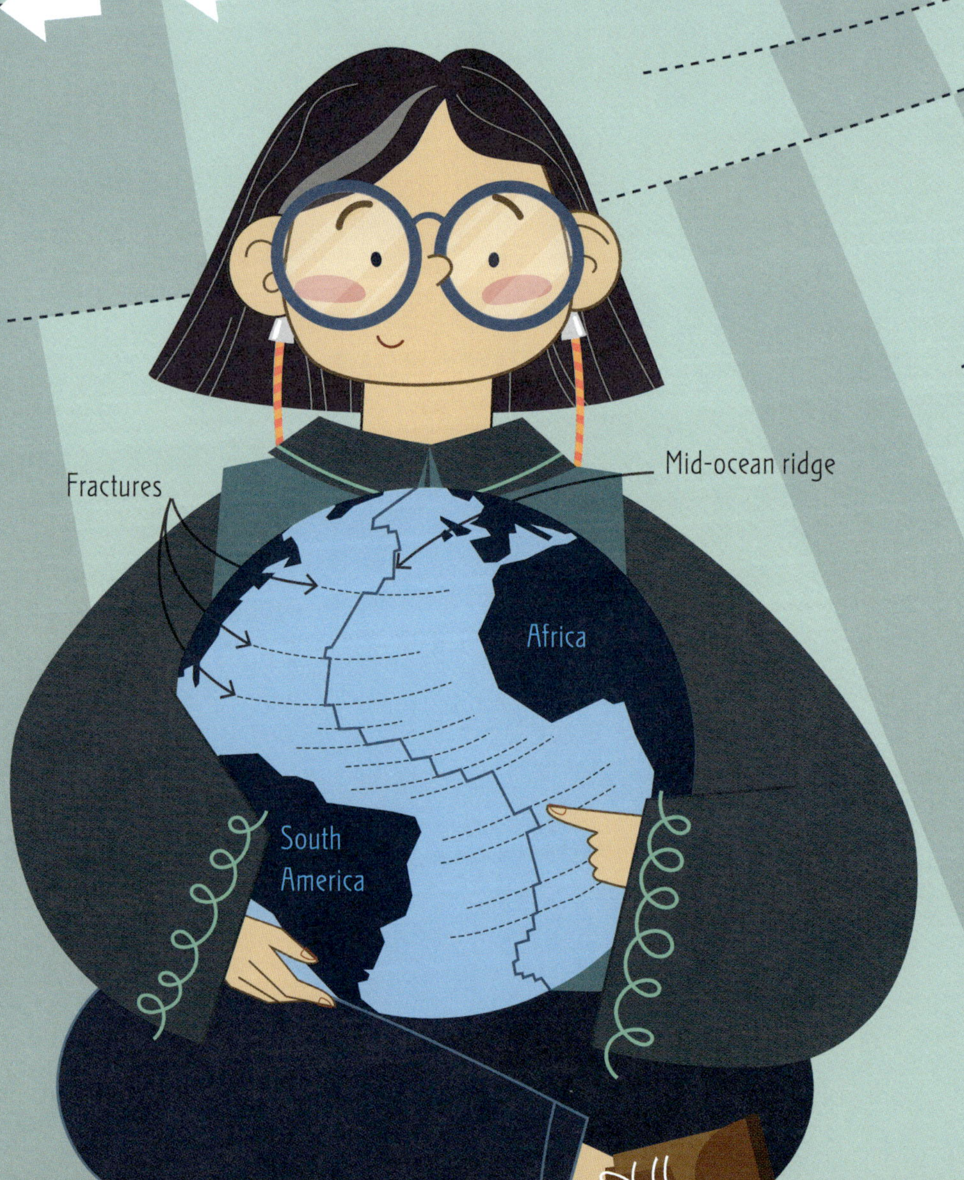

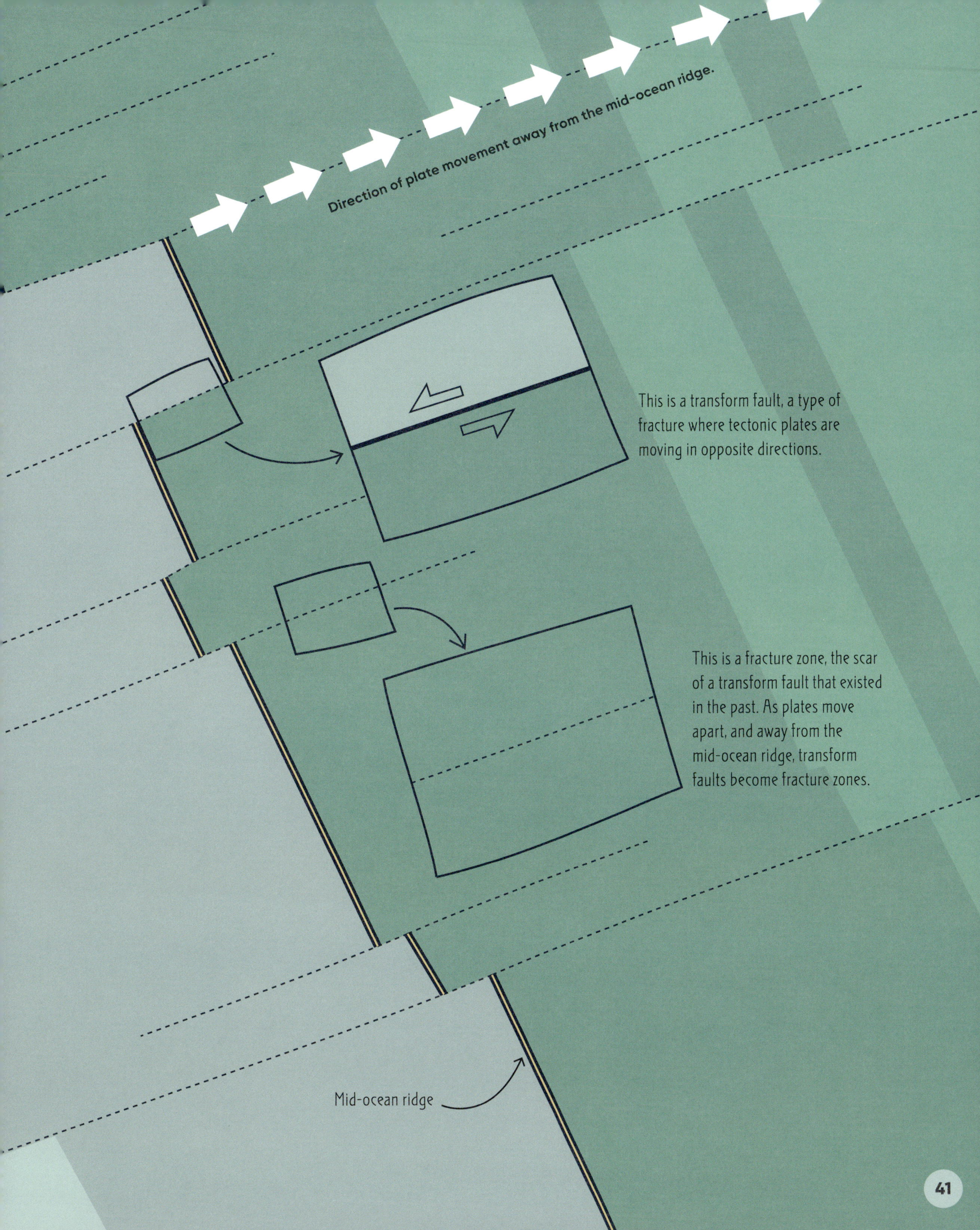
Direction of plate movement away from the mid-ocean ridge.
This is a transform fault, a type of fracture where tectonic plates are moving in opposite directions.
This is a fracture zone, the scar of a transform fault that existed in the past. As plates move apart, and away from the mid-ocean ridge, transform faults become fracture zones.
Mid-ocean ridge

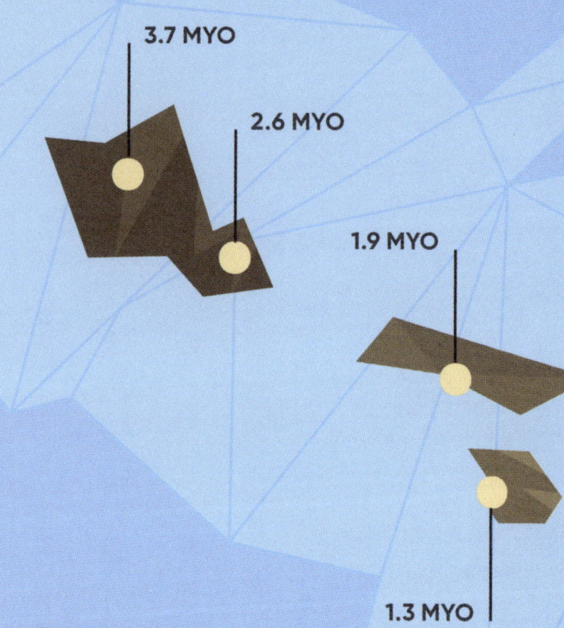

CONNECTING THE DOTS

Mid-ocean ridges and magnetic stripes are far from the only interesting things hiding beneath the waves. It's almost as if the Earth, as it evolved, was trying to leave us a trail of clues good enough for us to decipher the mystery of plate tectonics.

One of those clues comes in the form of island chains. In the middle of the Pacific Ocean, a dotted line of volcanic islands stretches toward the northwest from the island of Hawai'i. These islands were not all formed at once, and they are not aligned by accident.

They formed as the Pacific tectonic plate moved over a hot spot—a place where hot mantle rocks rise toward the surface. On Earth, most volcanoes form at plate boundaries, but hot spots are an exception. They create volcanoes away from the edges of plates.

Island chains show us which way the tectonic plate they're on is moving, but also how fast. In the case of the Hawaiian island chain, they tell us about the movements of the Pacific Plate during the last five million years.

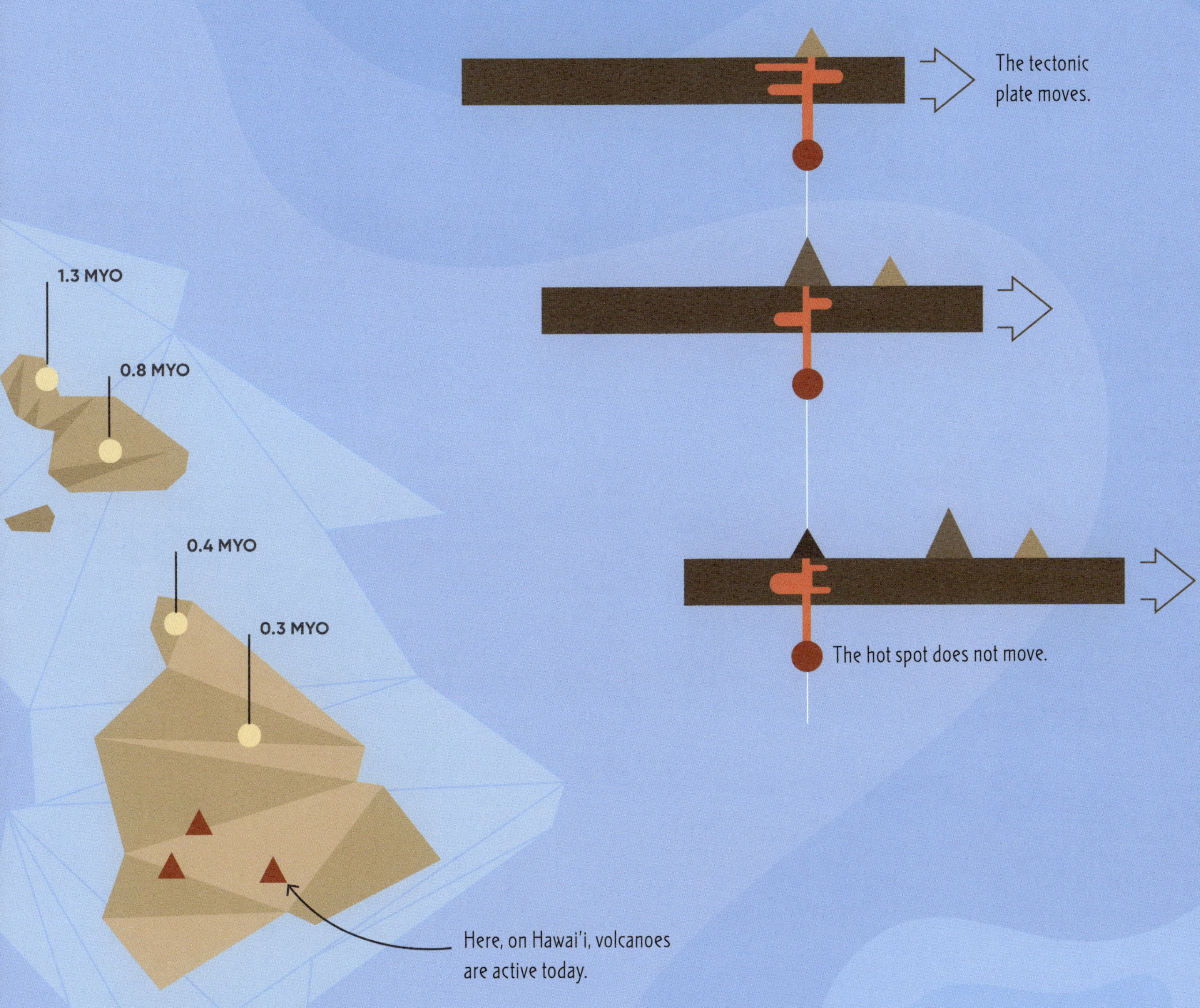

REWINDING THE PLATES

When we consider magnetic stripes, island chains, and fracture zones, the ocean floor is like a giant mystery waiting to be solved. It holds a record of what our planet looked like hundreds of millions of years ago. Earth scientists are like detectives. They gather these clues and use them to build plate reconstructions—maps of ancient Earth. No time machine needed: the history of the oceans is written under the water!

Plate reconstructions are like a jigsaw puzzle, but one where the pieces have changed shape over time. Imagine you were trying to find out what the South Atlantic Ocean looked like, 100 million years ago...

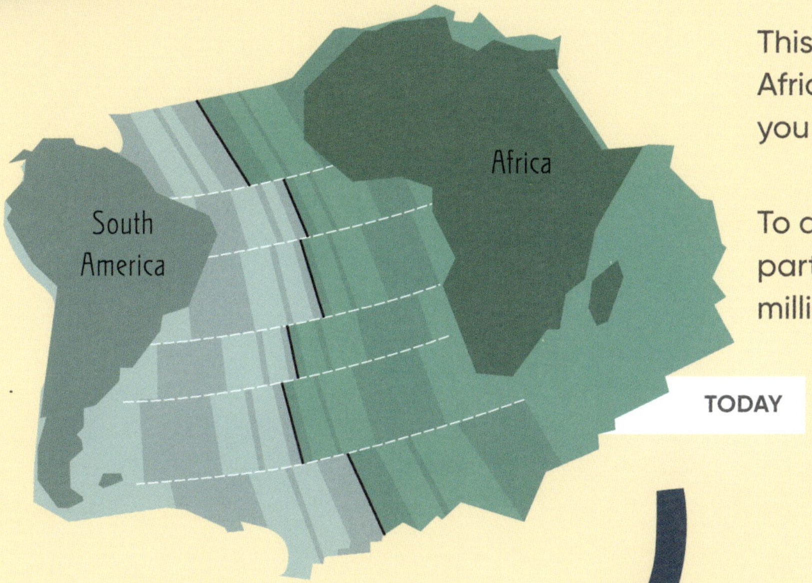

This is what the South American and African plates look like today. First, you would need to "reshape" them.

To do that, you would remove any part of the plates younger than 100 million years old.

This seafloor did not yet exist, 100 million years ago.

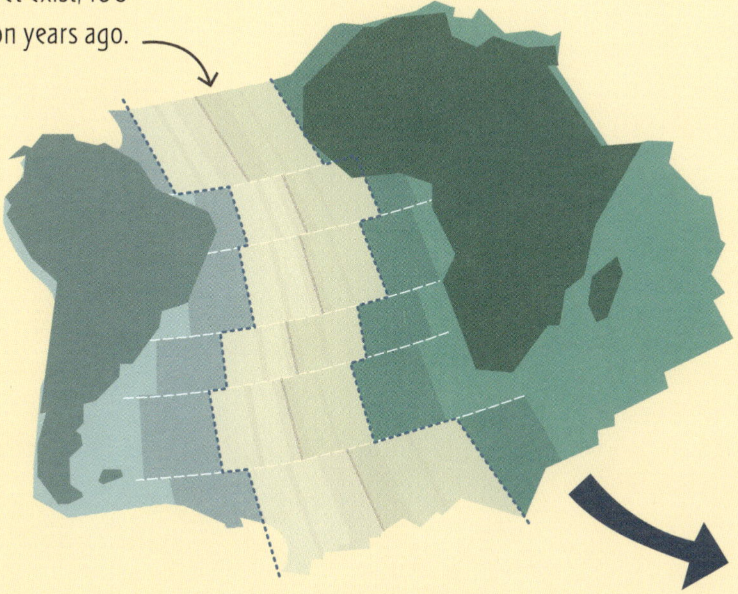

Thanks to magnetic stripes and fracture zones, redrawing the plates is quite easy.

Once you have cut away the parts of the plates you don't need, all that is left is to realign them.

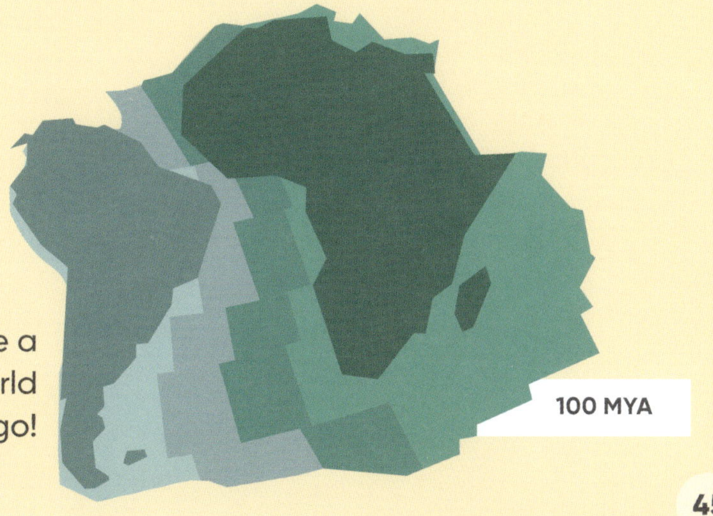

And just like that, you will have a picture of what this part of the world looked like 100 million years ago!

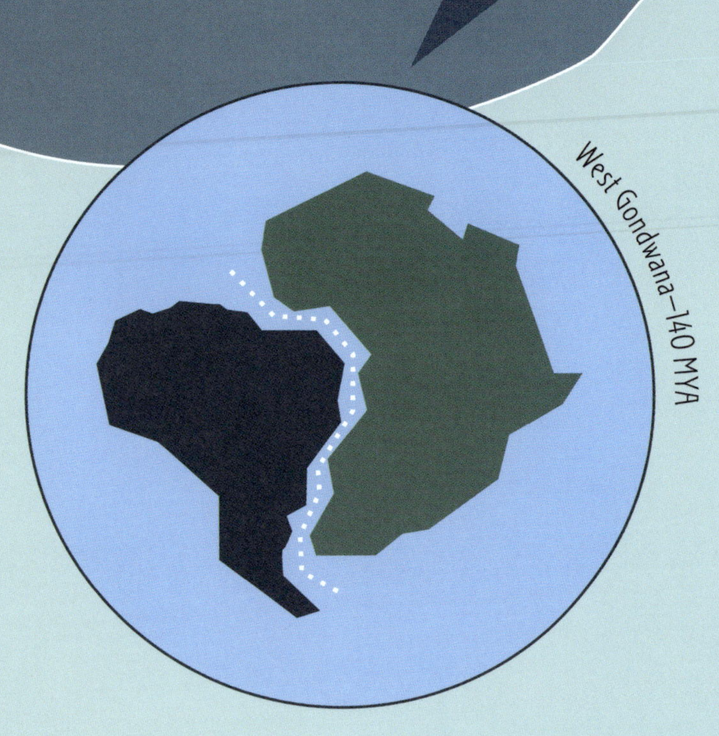

AN OCEAN COMES, AN OCEAN GOES

Using plate reconstruction, the story of the South Atlantic comes to life—its oldest seafloor is around 140 million years old, which means that, before that, South America and Africa were connected as part of a supercontinent: Gondwana. Then, they broke apart, and the South Atlantic Ocean grew between.

The same kind of detective work can be done for any of today's oceans. But there's a limit: we can only go back as far as the oldest surviving seafloor, roughly a couple of hundred millions of years. And yet, Earth is more than 4.6 billion years old. Oceans have existed for almost all of that time. So where is the rest of the story?

It's missing, because oceans eventually vanish.

In the North Atlantic, you can find oceanic lithosphere as old as 180 million years.
The oldest intact seafloor on Earth (that we know of) is in the Mediterranean, and is around 250 million years old.
The oldest seafloor in the South Atlantic is around 140 million years old.
Mid-Atlantic Ridge

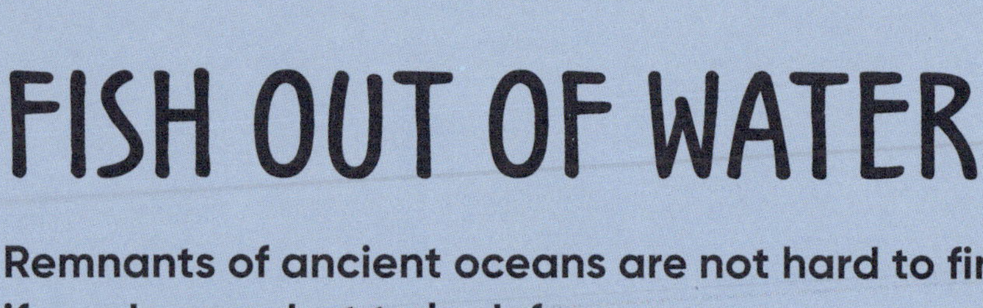

FISH OUT OF WATER

Remnants of ancient oceans are not hard to find, if you know what to look for.

High in the Himalayas, among snow and stone, explorers and scientists have found something strange: fish fossils. Sea creatures... in the world's tallest mountains. That shouldn't be possible, unless those rocks were once at the bottom of the ocean!

And they were.

Ophiolite

Fossilized fish

The fish fossils are just one clue. You can also find chunks of ancient oceanic lithosphere (known as ophiolite) up in the mountains.

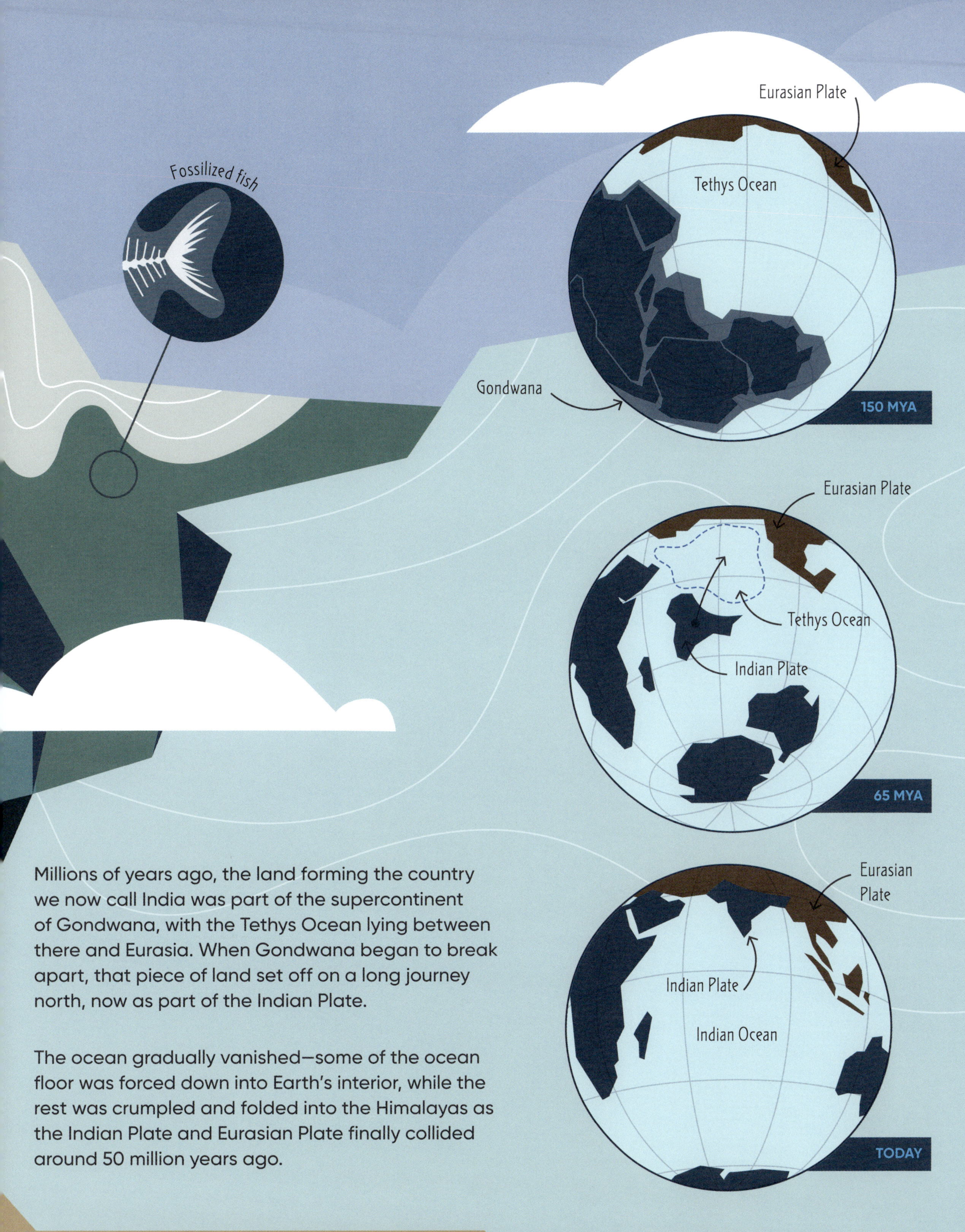

Millions of years ago, the land forming the country we now call India was part of the supercontinent of Gondwana, with the Tethys Ocean lying between there and Eurasia. When Gondwana began to break apart, that piece of land set off on a long journey north, now as part of the Indian Plate.

The ocean gradually vanished—some of the ocean floor was forced down into Earth's interior, while the rest was crumpled and folded into the Himalayas as the Indian Plate and Eurasian Plate finally collided around 50 million years ago.

EARTH'S RECYCLING BELT

The Tethys Ocean had no choice but to disappear because new lithosphere is constantly created at mid-ocean ridges, and the planet's surface would get crowded really quickly unless lithosphere is destroyed somewhere else.

Most tectonic plates are made up of two types of lithosphere: continental (the landmasses) and oceanic (the oceans). The type of lithosphere is what determines whether or not it eventually gets destroyed.

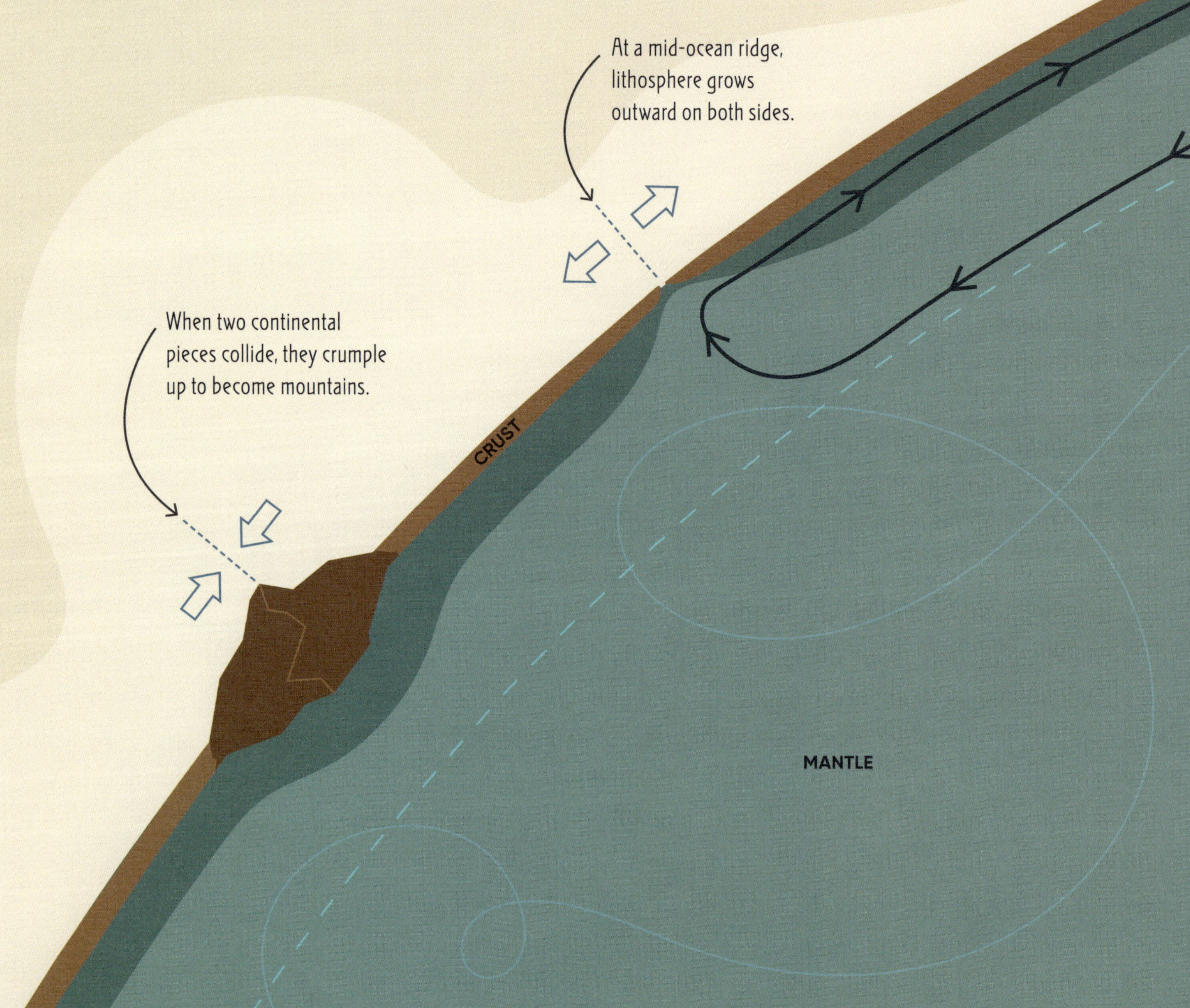

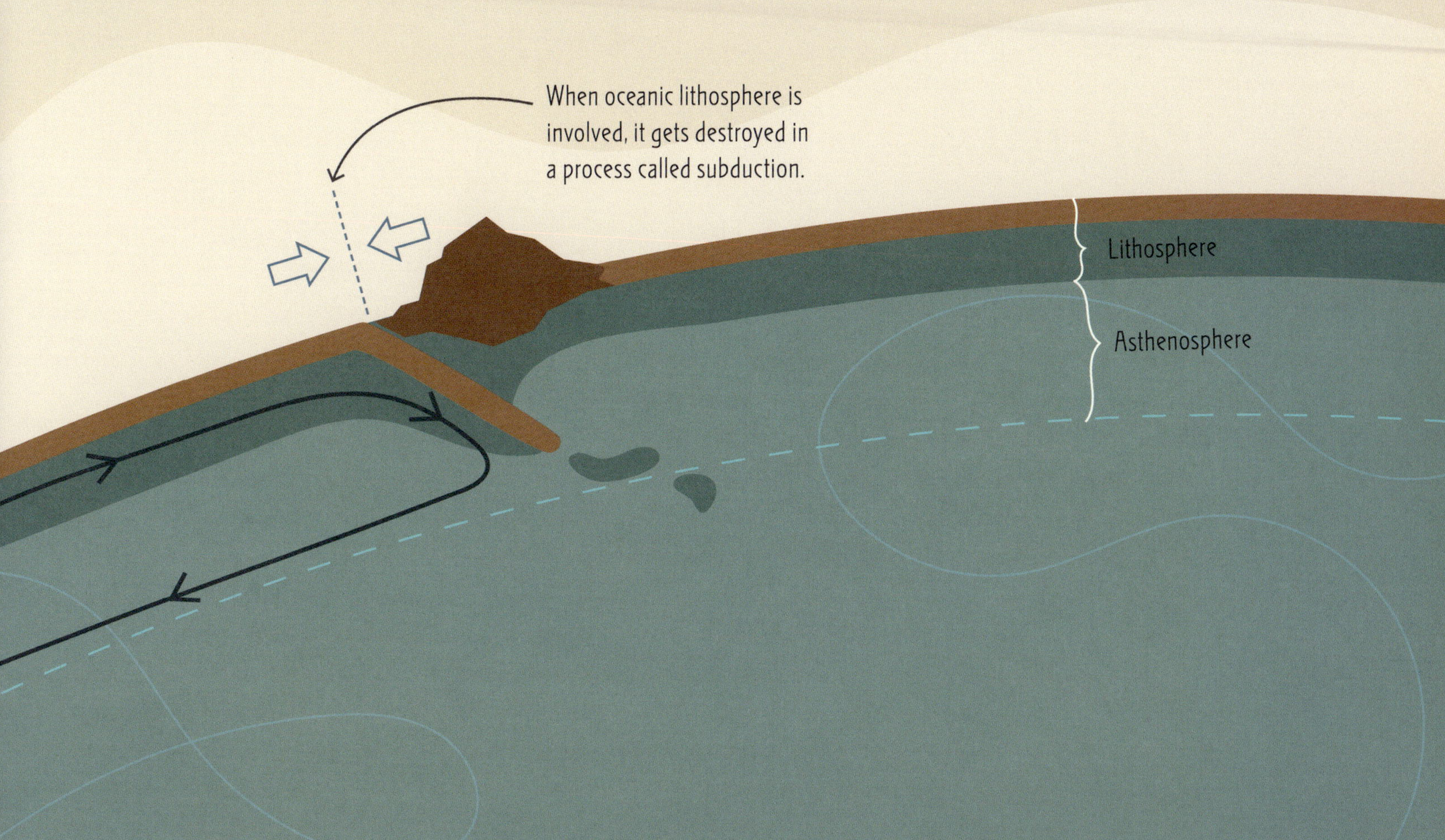

Oceanic lithosphere is heavy. Continental lithosphere is light. When the two meet, the denser oceanic plate sinks into the mantle beneath the continental plate. Subduction also happens when two oceanic plates collide. In that case, the older plate is usually the one sinking. Because of this constant recycling, ocean floors never last very long.

Continents, by contrast, are much older because they never subduct. When two continents collide, neither can sink. Instead, they crumple and fold, building great mountain chains, just like the Himalayas today.

It's easy to think of tectonic plates like puzzle pieces, but they're more like parts of a conveyor belt. Rocks from the mantle rise at mid-ocean ridges to form new lithosphere, and old lithosphere is recycled back into the planet's interior. Plates are built, moved, and destroyed—over and over again.

CORE

Even really big oceans will eventually disappear. Take the Pacific Ocean—the largest on Earth today, covering more than a third of the planet... But it is getting smaller every day.

All around the edges of the Pacific, subduction zones are at work. The Pacific Plate is being pulled under the plates around it. Earthquakes shake its borders. Volcanoes line up along its edge. This zone encircling the Pacific Ocean is so active, it's been nicknamed the Ring of Fire.

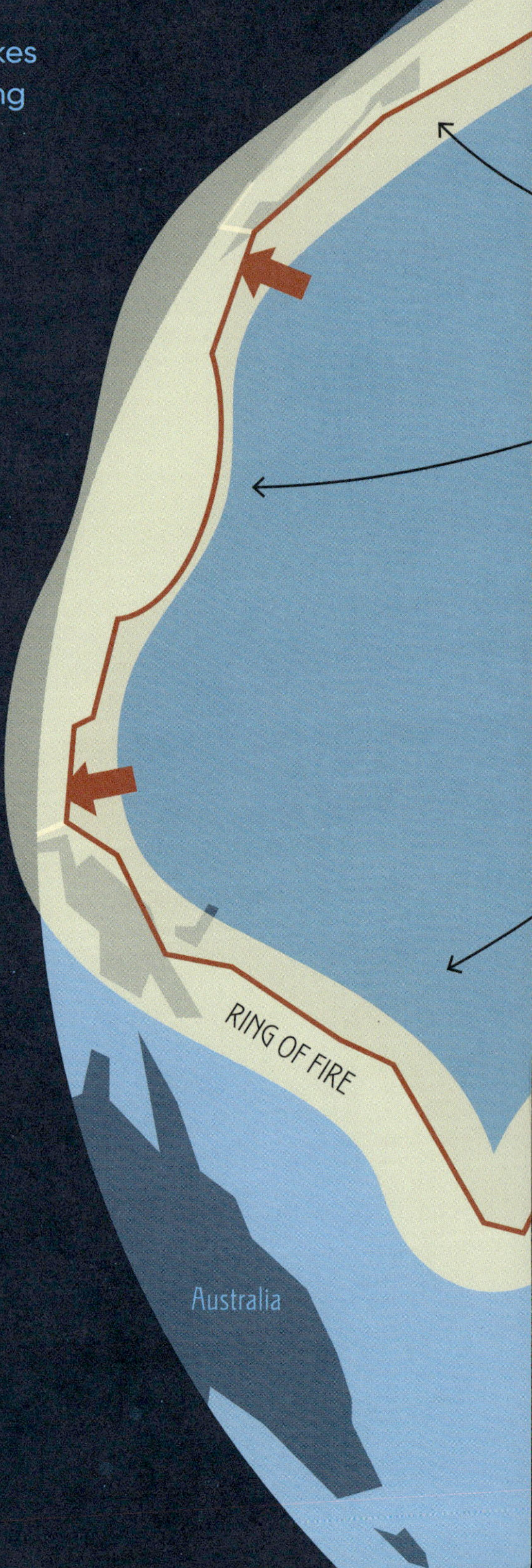

As more and more of the Pacific floor is swallowed up, the ocean slowly shrinks. In a few hundred million years, the Pacific could completely disappear, and it wouldn't be the first really big ocean to vanish.

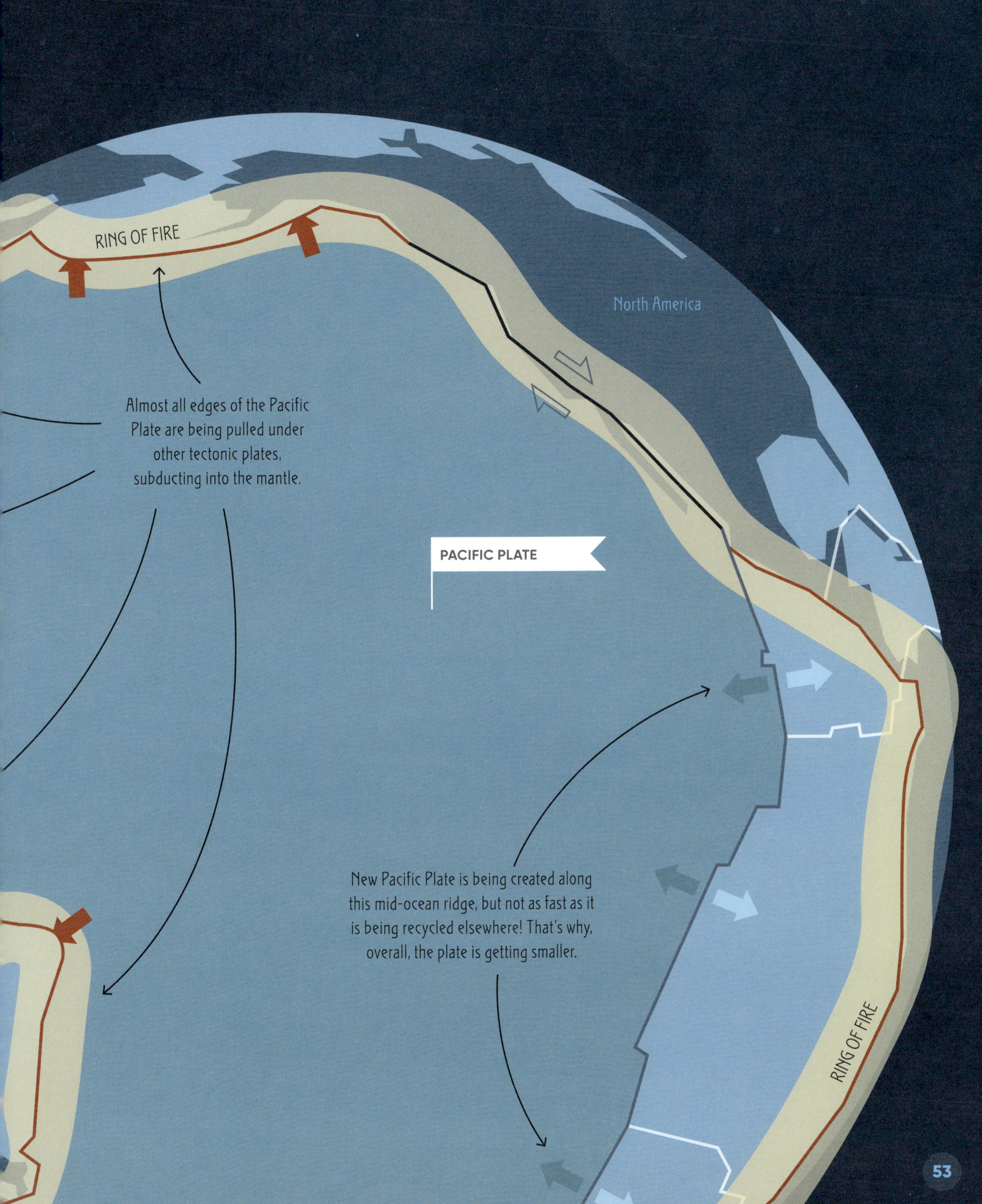
RING OF FIRE
North America
Almost all edges of the Pacific Plate are being pulled under other tectonic plates, subducting into the mantle.
PACIFIC PLATE
New Pacific Plate is being created along this mid-ocean ridge, but not as fast as it is being recycled elsewhere! That's why, overall, the plate is getting smaller.
RING OF FIRE

THE SUPEROCEAN THAT DISAPPEARED

Around 300 million years ago, all land on Earth was part of one single supercontinent: Pangea. And, around it, there was an ocean bigger than any on Earth today: Panthalassa. But, 200 million years ago, Pangea started breaking into different continents due to the movement of tectonic plates. Little by little, the world started changing. As the broken-up pieces drifted away from each other, new oceans formed. Panthalassa slowly vanished, most of it being subducted back into the mantle.

The Panthalassa Ocean was full of life.
It was home to lots of free-floating creatures like belemnites. They weren't big, scary monsters though! Most measured less than a few inches.

DEEP TIME

With so much evidence found today on the seafloor, reconstructing the motions of tectonic plates is relatively easy. But what if you want to look further back in time, before the oldest ocean crust we have?

It's a lot harder, but not impossible. Earth's memory, just like ours, is a little hazier the further back you go. When it comes to "deep time" (before today's oceans existed), plate reconstructions rely on clues that are less precise, but still valuable.

Scientists match up mountain ranges, fossil records, and rock types that have been found on now-distant continents, to find out which pieces of land used to be together.

They also use paleomagnetism, the study of the magnetic signals locked in ancient rocks, to help track where land masses were back in time.

Another clue is hidden in the Earth's mantle. Subducted slabs of oceanic lithosphere can be "desubducted" (pulled back up) in computer models, helping to estimate the size and location of ancient oceans.

It's still like putting a giant jigsaw puzzle together, but one with more missing and broken pieces the further back you go.

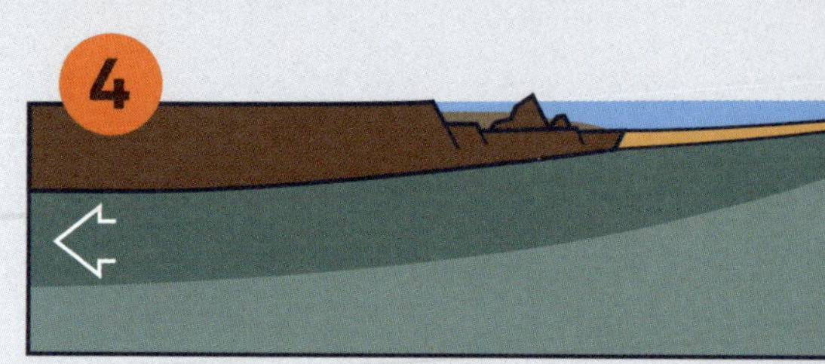

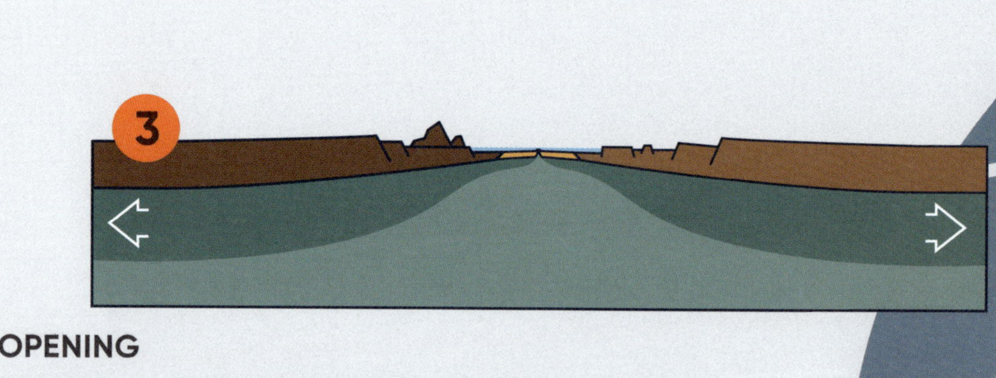

OPENING

The magma is exposed at the surface, cooling and forming new oceanic crust. This new crust, together with the top part of the mantle, becomes brand-new oceanic lithosphere—an ocean is born.

GROWING

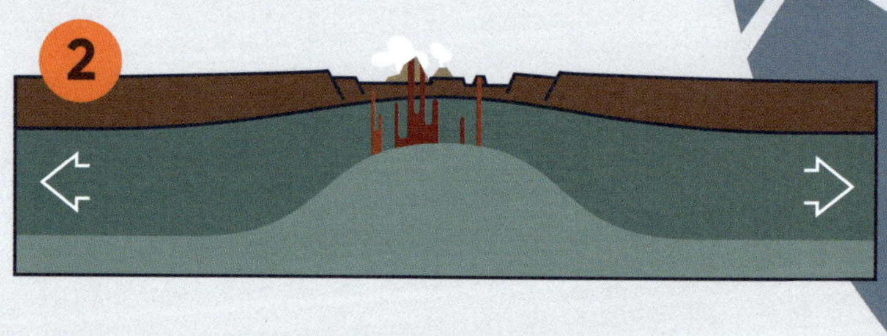

RIFTING

A continent pulls apart, stretching and cracking, like in East Africa today. The underlying asthenosphere rises, and mantle rocks start to melt as they rise and are brought closer to the surface.

THE OCEAN LIFE CYCLE

Oceans on Earth are born, evolve, and eventually die. This entire process has a name: the Wilson Cycle, named after the geologist J. Tuzo Wilson. It's the full life story of an ocean, from beginning to end.

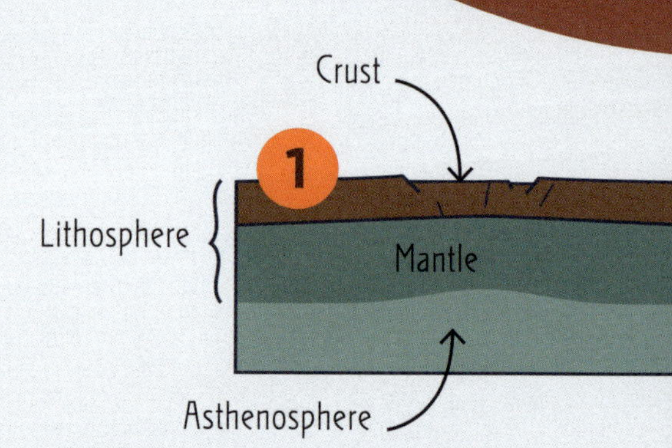

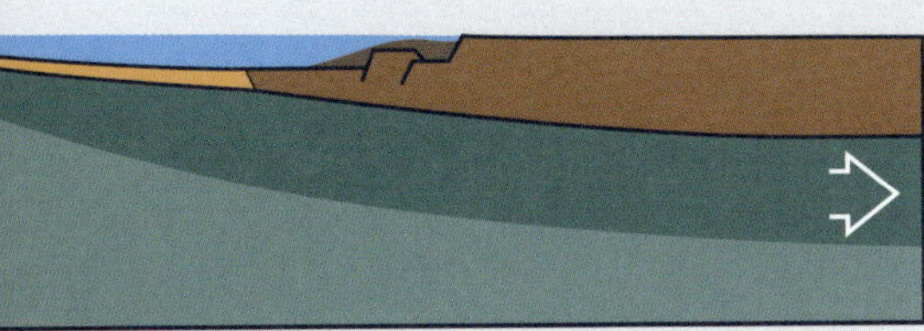

SPREADING

The ocean widens as the tectonic plates spread farther apart. As lithosphere gets older, away from the mid-ocean ridge, it becomes colder and more dense.

SHRINKING

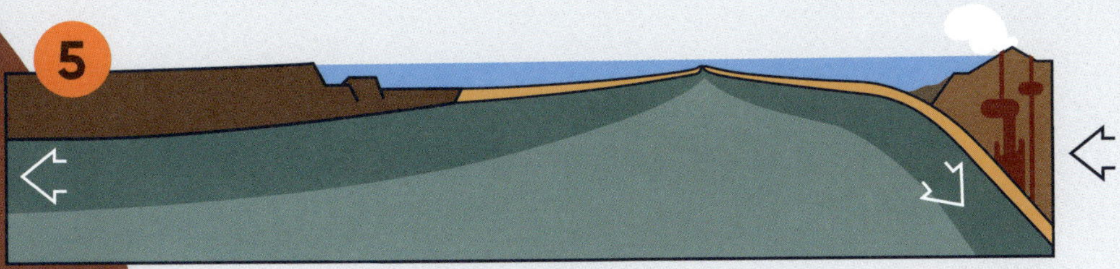

5

SUBDUCTION STARTS

Old and dense seafloor starts to sink back into the mantle over time, and a subduction zone forms.

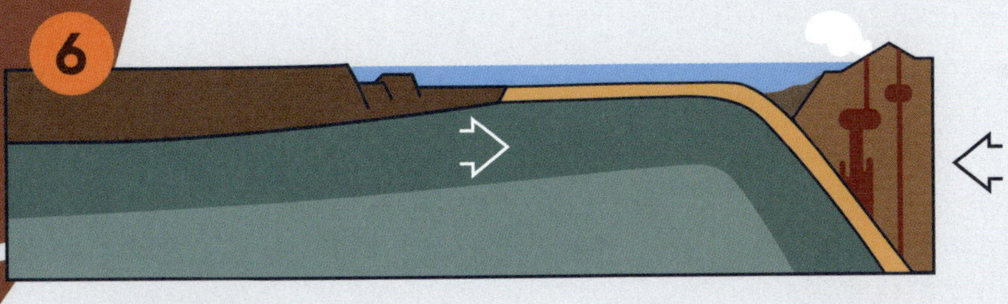

6

CLOSING

As more of the lithosphere is subducted, the ocean shrinks. Continents on either side of it move closer together.

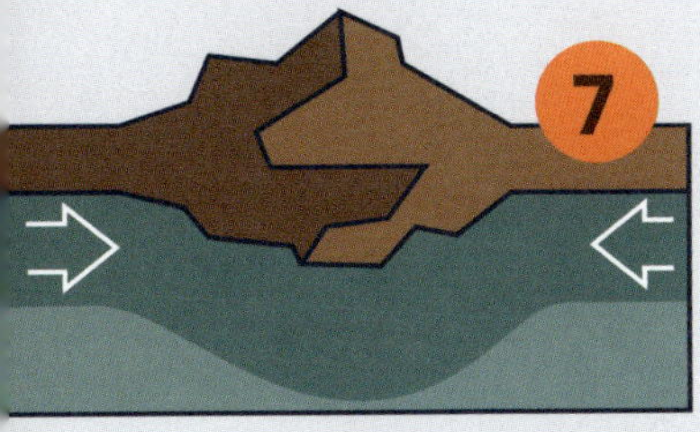

7

Eventually, continents collide and the last bits of ocean vanish. The whole cycle takes hundreds of millions of years to complete, and once it's over a new rift can start somewhere else... and the whole thing begins again.

JUST KEEP MOVING

New lithosphere is created at mid-ocean ridges and destroyed in subduction zones in a cycle that has been repeating for hundreds of millions of years. But what keeps the plate tectonic system moving? How did it all start, and when?

We don't have all the answers, but oceans seem to play a big role. Oceanic lithosphere is recycled back into Earth's mantle and, when it sinks, it creates a downward pulling force. This "slab pull" is thought to be the main force driving plate tectonics. The bigger the slab, the stronger the pull.

Because tectonic plates carry our continents as well as our oceans, this slab pull means that oceans are actually moving the ground beneath our feet. And the ways in which they influence our planet **go even further**...

A BROWN PLANET?

Imagine you woke up tomorrow and all the oceans were gone. No beaches, no waves, no salty air. And the changing landscape would be the least of your problems. Oceans supply most of the water vapor that forms clouds. Without them, clouds and rain would fade, the atmosphere would become thinner, and sunlight would hit the ground more directly.

Oceans are great at storing heat, soaking up warmth and releasing it slowly, which helps keep temperatures stable. They also absorb carbon dioxide from the air, regulating the amount of greenhouse gases in the atmosphere. Without oceans doing their job, temperatures would swing wildly between scorching heat and freezing cold. There would be nothing but bare deserts and icy wastelands, where life as we know it would struggle to survive.

Oceans don't just shape what Earth looks like, they are much more important than that. They rule the climate, keeping it just right for life to thrive.

EARTH'S THERMOSTAT

You can think of oceans as Earth's giant thermostat. They soak up energy from the sun and move it around the globe, helping to keep temperatures stable and weather patterns more predictable. This steady flow influences storms, rainfall, and seasonal temperature changes across the world.

Deep ocean currents act like a giant conveyor belt, carrying warm water from the tropics toward the poles, and sending cooler water back again.

How ocean water moves—and how it moved in the past—has a huge impact on Earth's weather and climate. By reconstructing the motions of tectonic plates, and how they shaped oceans over time, scientists can not only see what Earth looked like, but also understand what it *was* like. Reconstructing the past helps us understand how ocean currents once flowed, how they shaped ancient climates, and what changes might lie ahead.

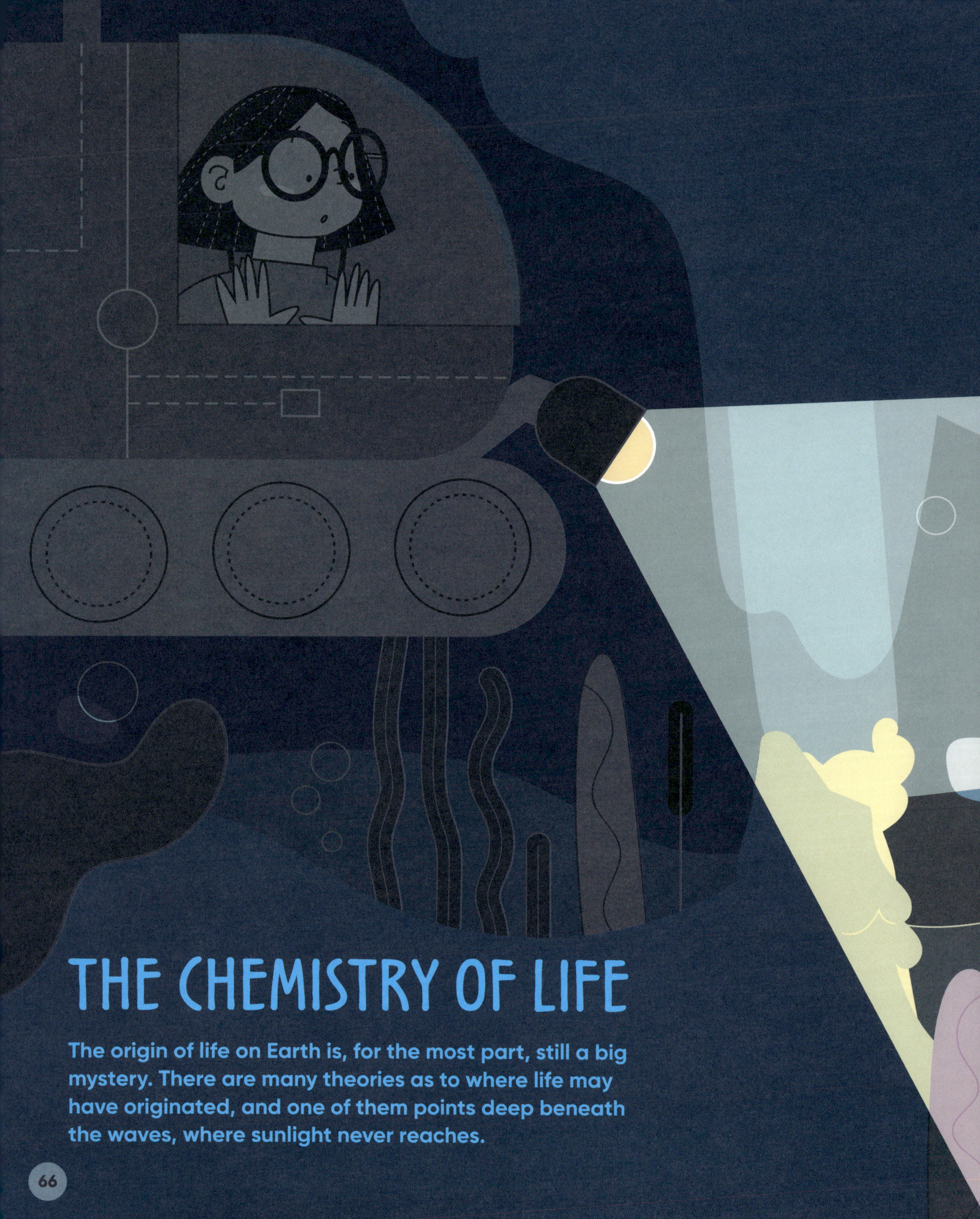

THE CHEMISTRY OF LIFE

The origin of life on Earth is, for the most part, still a big mystery. There are many theories as to where life may have originated, and one of them points deep beneath the waves, where sunlight never reaches.

Near mid-ocean ridges and subduction zones, water sinks down through cracks in the seafloor and into the hot mantle. There, it heats up, before reemerging back up to form something called a hydrothermal vent. This hot water carries gases like hydrogen and methane, and elements like iron and sulfur. Scientists think that these compounds can act as the building blocks for organic molecules (in other words, life).

When scientists first discovered hydrothermal vents, they were shocked by the variety of never-before-seen organisms living around them, which supports the idea that these are places where life can thrive.

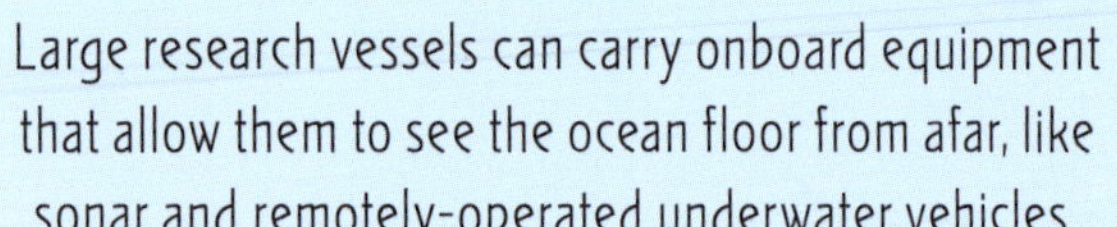

A HIDDEN WORLD

Under thousands of feet of water, below the abyssal zone, the deepest ocean is dark, freezing cold, and the water above is so heavy it can crush almost anything. Exploring it is like visiting another planet! Building submarines to reach these depths is really tricky, so only a few humans have ever visited the very deepest parts.

Because diving so deep is so dangerous, scientists often send robots instead. Satellites and sonar equipment can map the seafloor from above, while autonomous underwater vehicles can dive deep, collect samples, and send pictures back. Each research mission teaches us more about this strange, hidden world.

Even satellites can be used to map the ocean floor, all the way from outer space!

660 ft (200 m)

The sunlight zone

The twilight zone

3,280 ft (1,000 m)

The midnight zone

13,120 ft (4,000 m)

The abyssal zone

19,685 ft (6,000 m)

The hadal zone

36,090 ft (11,000 m)

The deepest place we know is Challenger Deep, nearly 36,090 ft (11,000 m) down in the Mariana Trench, a subduction zone. It was first measured in 1875 using a rope with a weight on the end... A very, very long rope.

In 2019, humans managed the deepest dive to date, reaching a depth of 35,853 ft (10,928 m).

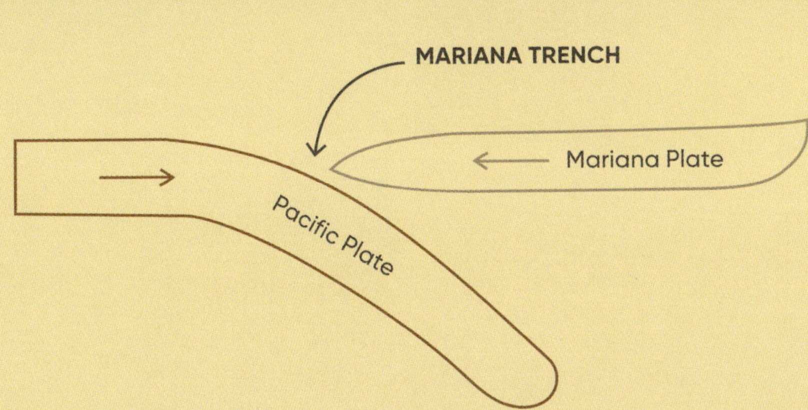

The Mariana Trench is part of the subduction zone where the Pacific Plate is sinking underneath the Mariana Plate, in the Pacific Ocean.

OCEANS FAR AWAY

Earth's oceans have shown us that life can exist in extreme environments, so it's not unreasonable to think that there may be oceans on other planets—and that life may exist within them. If we do find life, it may teach us a lot about the early stages of the evolution of life on Earth.

The first place we looked at was Mars. It's smaller than Earth and farther from the sun, but its surface is marked by dried-up riverbeds and ancient lake beds—evidence that water once flowed there. Today, water only exists in the form of frozen ice, at its poles. So far, we haven't found signs of life, but the search isn't over.

Also promising are the icy moons of the outer solar system. Europa, one of Jupiter's moons, and Enceladus, which orbits Saturn, are both frozen on the outside—but beneath their icy crusts may lie vast, salty oceans. These oceans are trapped in darkness, but they might be kept warm under the ice, by energy from within these faraway worlds.

On Enceladus, scientists have even seen giant water plumes erupting through cracks in the ice, like geysers. These eruptions suggest there's liquid water within, and an energy source—two key ingredients for life.

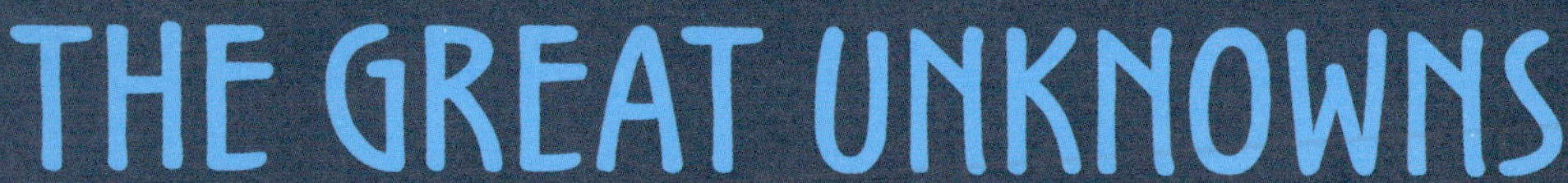

THE GREAT UNKNOWNS

It's amazing how much we've discovered about Earth thanks to the oceans. They show us what the planet looked like in the past, may have sparked the first life, and help keep it habitable today.

But even though oceans cover 70 percent of the planet, we've only mapped about 25 percent of their floors in detail, and explored less than 5 percent of their deepest parts. That means more than 95 percent of the deep ocean is still a mystery.

What strange life forms might be lurking in those dark depths? What clues about Earth's history have yet to be discovered? Considering what we've already learned, just imagine what's still waiting to be found.

The story of Earth's oceans is over 4 billion years old—and it's still unfolding. Studying the oceans has helped us uncover incredible things, but what answers may still be hiding deep under the waves? Science is all about curiosity: asking questions no one has asked before.

Will you help uncover the next chapter of the oceans' story?

GLOSSARY

ASTHENOSPHERE
soft, flowing part of the mantle found below the lithosphere

ATMOSPHERE
layer of gases surrounding a planet

CHALLENGER DEEP
deepest known place in the ocean, part of the Mariana Trench subduction zone

CONTINENTAL
relating to continents

CONVERGENT BOUNDARY
boundary where two tectonic plates are colliding. At this type of boundary, either one plate subducts under the other (sinks beneath), or both plate edges are pushed together to form mountains

CORE
central layer of the Earth, made up mostly of metal

CRUST
Earth's thin, rocky outer layer

DEEP TIME
times far in the past, before the formation of Earth's present day oceans

DIVERGENT BOUNDARY
boundary where two tectonic plates are moving apart and new rock is being created

FRACTURE ZONE
scar left on the seafloor by a transform fault that existed in the past

FRESH WATER
water containing little to no salt

GEOMAGNETIC TIMESCALE
calendar of magnetic field flips in the planet's past, stretching back millions of years

GREENHOUSE GASES
gases in the atmosphere that trap heat from the sun

GROUNDWATER
water stored underground in soil and rocks

HOTSPOT
point where hot rock from deep inside the mantle rises toward the surface of the Earth

HOMO SAPIENS
scientific name for modern humans

HYDROTHERMAL VENT
crack on the seabed from which superheated water shoots out

LITHOSPHERE
Earth's hard outer layer, including the crust and top of the mantle

MAGMA
molten (liquid or semiliquid) rock located under Earth's surface. When magma comes to the surface, it is called lava

MAGNETIC FIELD
area of magnetism surrounding a magnet or a planetary body

MAGNETOMETER
instrument measuring the strength and direction of a magnetic field

MANTLE
layer of the Earth between the crust and the core

MID-OCEAN RIDGE
underwater chain of volcanoes, where tectonic plates are moving away from each other and new seafloor is being created

OCEAN CURRENT
a flow of ocean water that moves warm or cold water around the world

OCEANIC
relating to oceans

OPHIOLITE
ancient pieces of oceanic crust, found on land

PALEOMAGNETISM
study of magnetic minerals trapped inside ancient rocks

PILLOW BASALT
rock that forms when lava erupts underwater

PLATE RECONSTRUCTION
map of ancient Earth

REVERSE POLARITY
phenomenon where Earth's normal magnetic field flips, so the magnetic north becomes the magnetic south

RIFTING
process where a tectonic plate begins to split apart

RING OF FIRE
zone around the Pacific Plate where most of the world's volcanoes are found

SLAB PULL
downward pulling force created when a piece of oceanic lithosphere is recycled back into the Earth, thought to be the main force driving plate tectonics

SUBDUCTION
when one tectonic plate sinks beneath another

SUPERCONTINENT
huge landmass covering part of the Earth

TECTONIC PLATE
piece of the Earth's lithosphere

THERMOSTAT
device used to regulate temperature

TRANSFORM FAULT
fracture in the seafloor on either side of a mid-ocean ridge, where different tectonic plates slide past each other—a type of transform plate boundary

TRANSFORM PLATE BOUNDARY
boundary where two plates slide past each other without making or destroying rock

WATER CYCLE
the never-ending movement of water on Earth

WILSON CYCLE
the long life story of an ocean—how it opens, grows, and closes

INDEX

O

P

R

S

T

V

W

Z

Author and illustrator Dr. Lucía Pérez Díaz
Consultant Graeme Eagles

Project Editor Abi Maxwell
US Editor Jane Perlmutter
US Senior Editor Shannon Beatty
Senior Designer Laura Gardner
Managing Art Editor Anna Hall
Associate Publisher Gemma Far
Production Editor Gillian Reid
Senior Production Controller Ena Matagic

First American Edition, 2026
Published in the United States by DK Publishing,
a division of Penguin Random House LLC
1745 Broadway, 20th Floor, New York, NY 10019

26 27 28 29 30 10 9 8 7 6 5 4 3 2 1
001–354981–July/2026

Published in Great Britain by Dorling Kindersley Limited

ISBN 979-8-2171-3410-6

This book was made with Forest Stewardship Council™ certified paper – one small step in DK's commitment to a sustainable future.
Learn more at www.dk.com/uk/information/sustainability

ACKNOWLEDGMENTS

The publisher would like to thank:

Claire Sipi for proofreading, Vanessa Bird for the index, and Amy Child for design assistance.

From Lucía:

To my wonderful agent Gill (and her canine assistant Gatsby) at the Bath Literary Agency, thank you for your continued support, wise advice, and for always being willing to listen to my sometimes slightly wacky book ideas.

Many people around me have once again very generously gifted their time by reading drafts of this book, commenting on the artwork, and patiently acting as sounding boards throughout the process. In particular, I would like to thank Kirstie, Meghan, and Graeme. And of course, my brilliant DK family—especially Laura, Abi, Anna, and Gemma—thank you for your guidance in making the content engaging and accessible, and for indulging my need to trial what felt like endless shades of blue until the right ones finally revealed themselves.

Lastly, I must thank my youngest advisors, Magnus and Margot, who have kept my drawing skills sharp by regularly challenging me to draw things I would never think of on my own. Keep drawing, and don't let growing up get in the way of your imagination.